Counted-Thread Embroidery

HELEN FAIRFIELD

Counted-Thread Embroidery

with illustrations by the author

St. Martin's Press · New York

LIBRARY OF CONGRESS CATALOG CARD NUMBER: 87-42636
ISBN 0-312-01236-5

First published in Great Britain by B.T. Batsford Ltd.
First U.S. Edition.

10 9 8 7 6 5 4 3 2 1

Photographs by Peter Haines
Typeset by Servis Filmsetting Ltd., Manchester

Dedicated to the memory of my grandmother,
May Campbell Nixon
London, England, 1868 – Saskatchewan, Canada, 1962,
who passed on to me her love of
embroidery

Contents

Introduction

Whether one studies and works towards examinations and qualifications in embroidery oneself, or prepares lesson notes to teach the subject, the need to haunt libraries to search out fugitive references in order to track down elusive yet vital facts can be both time-consuming and frustrating. This is especially true when a particular field of embroidery has no books available devoted solely to it, but references must be sought under many headings and in many journals.

During the years I taught in comprehensive schools in north-west London I felt a particular need for a book covering all the various types of embroidery which are worked by counting threads on evenweave fabrics. Apart from one rather limited book published in 1955, I was unable to find any, so I assembled lesson notes to supplement the text books which, except for such popular skills as cross stitch and canvas work, blackwork and pulled thread, were often inadequate or non-existent. When early retirement gave me the leisure to do so, it seemed a good idea to turn these notes into the book I had been looking for. If I had felt such a need, perhaps there were others who shared it.

The more one studies, the wider the field becomes. When I taught teenagers in secondary schools there was no need to know more than that work with a cross stitch background, the figure being voided, was known as Assisi work. I soon learned that there are embroideries from all over the world which, under their own regional names, fit this description, but unless I let each chapter expand to book length, there is no room for such fascinating information here. If your pet exotic embroidery is missing from these pages, please understand. Where possible, I have tried to give, at the end of each chapter, a book list which will enable the interested reader to follow such trails further. Except for a few exceptional books, long out of print, the titles given should all be available through a good public library.

For the most part, the books listed have been my sources, together with stacks of *Embroidery* magazine going back thirty years, which I cherish. I am most grateful for the privilege of being allowed the freedom of the splendid libraries at the London College of Fashion, and the Embroiderers' Guild, and access to the embroidery collections at the Victoria & Albert Museum and the Embroiderers' Guild. Without their help this would have been a much more difficult book to write.

ONE

Materials and equipment

Embroidery on evenweave linen has a history almost as old as the history of weaving. When the earliest people dressed themselves in skins, they probably decorated their clothing, as did the Innuit and the American Indian in well documented times, with appliqué and patchwork of different-coloured leathers and furs, with 'beading' of porcupine quills, or with free stitchery in sinews and grasses.

Once thread was spun and woven into cloth, embroidery over the counted threads of the new fabrics cannot have been far behind, and almost certainly came before patterned weaving. Unfortunately, because of the perishable nature of woven cloth, we can only guess at the antiquity of the stitches we practise, although there are specimens of cross stitch more than a thousand years old, and traditions hold that it is very much older. On walls in what was once Chaldea and Assyria are patterns which some believe imitate embroidery patterns in cross stitch. It has also been suggested that the geometric patterns on floors in Rome and Venice were copied from embroidery patterns rather than the other way around. (See *Needlework as Art*, Lady Mary Alford, 1886.)

The earliest documented embroideries on woven fabric were known as *opus pluvinarium*, or 'cushioned work'. The term embraced all kinds of embroidery which could be used on cushions and couches subject to heavy wear. Today we would term these embroideries cross stitch or canvas work.

Nearly as old are the types of embroidery which require the drawing out of some of the threads of the fabric to form a ground on which to work lacy patterns, or which rely on the displacement of the woven threads to provide decoration.

Today, because almost all the fabrics available to the embroiderer are manufactured on power looms, and have a stronger and heavier warp thread than that used for the weft, it is necessary to be very careful when selecting fabrics to work on. Even the expensive fabrics manufactured specially for embroidery, and supposedly 'evenweave', are not necessarily so, and it can be most annoying to work a piece of embroidery only to find that the 'square' of a cross stitch has been distorted into an oblong. As long as the design runs all in one direction the fault may not be too obvious, but where it extends round four sides of a cloth, it can be most disconcerting.

As an example. the two pigs in *fig. 1* meet at the corner of a cloth. They are identical, but reversed, and when embroidered on evenweave linen, should have the same proportions. *Fig. 2* shows what happens when the warp thread of the fabric is heavier than the weft, and the cross stich is pulled out of square.

It really is essential, therefore, to check the fabric before you start work. To do this, tack a horizontal and a vertical line on the fabric, using threads which contrast with the fabric, and making sure that the tacking stitches run along the line of a thread in the fabric. Measuring very carefully, make a rectangle by tacking two more lines, parallel to, but 5 cm (2 in) from the original tacked lines. Now count the

1

2

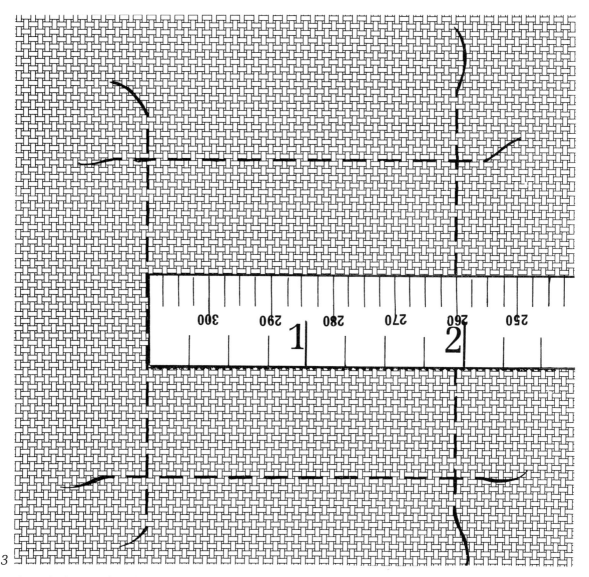

3

threads thus enclosed, vertically and horizontally (*fig. 3*). If these counts are the same, the fabric may be called 'evenweave', and used with confidence. If one count is larger than the other it may still be usable, but there will be some distortion of the stitches.

Evenweave fabrics sold for embroidery are mostly made of pure linen. This is strong, hardwearing and has a very pleasant lustre which is unmistakable. It is certainly the best fabric to use for most evenweave embroideries, but it is expensive.

Cheaper materials are manufactured in cotton for use in embroidery, but as they do not wear so well, nor have the 'handle' of the linen, they are best left for beginners to make their mistakes upon.

Evenweave woollen cloth is specially produced for embroidery. Such fabrics are useful for embroidery on dress, but are even more expensive than evenweave linen.

Very fine silk gauze is made for very fine canvas work embroidery in silk threads (petit point). Occasionally it is possible to find coarsely woven silks which have an even warp and weft.

There are a number of much cheaper materials available on fabric counters which are evenly woven or nearly so. It is worth investigating fine woollen dress fabrics, certain furnishing fabrics, and curtain nets, as well as hessians and scrims.

Today, canvas work is almost always worked on purpose-made linen or cotton canvas treated with a filler to stiffen it. Originally, the stitches were worked on a sort of linen scrim, and there is no reason why such a fabric should not be used if the work in hand requires it. Recently a plastic 'canvas' has come on to the market. This is not a woven material, but a pressing made to imitate linen canvas. Being very stiff, it is useful for constructions, or for articles like spectacle cases which would otherwise need a stiffened lining.

Originally, embroidery on linen fabric was worked with linen threads, but today, with linen threads difficult to come by in a wide range of colours, their use is restricted mainly to drawn thread and pulled thread work, and not necessarily used in those. Most fine embroidery today is done with fine cotton threads, either stranded or made into thin cord, while silk threads are available for special work which justifies the added expense. Canvas work is more likely to be worked with woollen threads, though cotton or silk may be used for special effects.

The needles used are almost always 'tapestry' needles (*fig. 4*) which have a large eye and a blunt point. The larger the needle, the smaller the number. The very fine No. 26 needles are desirable for fine work. When working in silk on silk gauze, I use a No. 11 or No. 12 crewel needle with the sharp point stoned till it is blunt and smooth. For work on canvas, a No. 20 or 22 tapestry needle would be used.

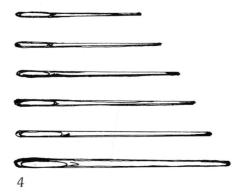

4

The general rule when working evenweave embroidery is that the needle should not be so large as to distort the weave of the ground fabric, and that the thread should match the threads of the ground fabric in weight and thickness. Obviously, there are exceptions where special effects are required, but this forms a good rule of thumb. Threads used should never be longer than 35 cm (14 in.), as a longer thread will wear and fuzz with the constant pulling through the fabric. Some threads need to be even shorter – experience will tell.

You will need a pair of dressmaking shears to cut your fabric but, more important, you will need a pair of fine, sharp embroidery scissors. They need not be so decorative as the ones shown in *fig. 5*, but it is a false economy to purchase cheap embroidery scissors. Do not use them for anything else. Particularly, do not use them to cut paper or plastic sheet! Have a special pair of paper cutting scissors for that.

5

I find a thimble essential for most kinds of evenweave embroidery. If you have not used one before, it may take some time to get used to it, but once wearing a thimble has become a habit it is an indispensable tool. Be sure to get a thimble which fits properly. Too loose, a thimble will fall off. Too tight, and it will hurt your finger in a very short time.

6

All embroidery on evenweave fabric benefits from being worked in a frame, which will keep the fabric in tension and the weave square while the stitches are being made. For some types of embroidery a frame is essential. It is best to get into the habit of using a frame for all your embroidery.

There are two types of frame, most people being familiar with the round or tambour frame. This is a full hoop of wood or plastic over which another hoop is fitted to clamp the fabric in position. The top hoop has been cut, and the cut ends are held together by a screw which is tightened to hold the fabric and loosened to release it.

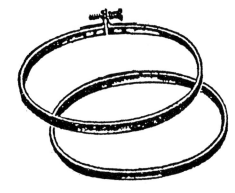

7

The tambour frame can be transported easily, and is simple to pack away when not in use. It does have some serious faults, however. It tends to mark the fabric, and it is difficult to keep the fabric taut when working. These faults can both be overcome to some degree by binding the inner ring with bias binding and sewing down the ends.

A more serious difficulty is that it is necessary to hold the frame in one hand and work with the other. With some techniques this can be quite a handicap. A frame which can be clamped to a table (*fig.8*) or has a base on which one can sit, gets around this particular problem.

Generally, a tambour frame would be used only for a small piece of work.

Much more satisfactory are the rectangular frames, sometimes known as slate frames.

These come in many varieties and sizes, but they all have two horizontal bars on to which webbing is fastened, and two vertical arms which hold these bars apart by the required distance. The cheapest version has four flat pieces of wood with holes

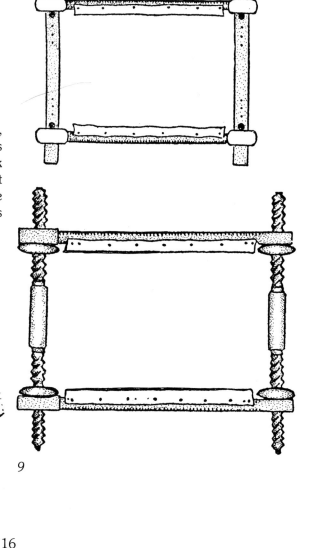

9

8

16

drilled at each end of each piece. The frame is assembled by inserting short bolts through the appropriate holes and fastening nuts on to them tightly. When the embroidery is mounted in the frame this arrangement is supposed to keep the frame square, but only too often this is not the case, and the frame pulls out of true, distorting the work. It is much better to spend a little more money and get a frame where the sides are rigid, as in *fig. 9*.

Slate frames can be held on the knee and propped against a table, or else rested on trestles. In either case it is possible to use both hands on the embroidery.

Even better is the frame shown in *fig. 10*, which is mounted on its own support.

Having gone to the trouble and expense of getting a good frame, and having chosen a piece of expensive linen to work on, it is important to know how to dress a frame properly.

First of all, find the centre of the webbing on the top and the bottom arms of your frame. Mark these points clearly and permanently.

Take your linen and fold it in half vertically. Crease the fold and then tack the line of the crease with contrasting thread, following the grain of the fabric carefully.

Fold a small hem on the top edge of the linen, and stitch it to the top arm of the frame, matching up the centre of the webbing to the centre line you have tacked on the linen. Sew out to the edges from the centre of the webbing, using herringbone stitch (*fig. 11*), and keeping the edges straight. Do the same on the bottom arm of the frame.

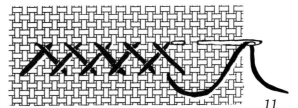

11

If your linen is longer than the frame allows for, remove the bottom bar of the frame to stitch the linen to the webbing, and then wind the excess linen around the bar before replacing it on the frame. Tighten the linen on the frame until you have the tension you require.

The sides may be tensioned either by tacking a hem on the sides of the linen, and threading cord

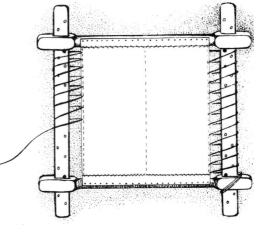

10

12

17

through it and around the side member of the frame, or by sewing tape to the sides of the linen with herringbone stitches, and taking the tensioning cord through that (*fig. 12*).

Ensure that the warp and weft threads of the linen are at right angles to each other before the final tension is applied.

If an awkward shape, or a very small piece of precious silk gauze, is to be mounted in a frame, dress the frame first with a piece of calico or cotton sheeting. When all is taut and the threads of warp and weft are at right angles, lay the small piece of fabric on the dressed frame and pin into place with very fine pins or needles. Check that the grain of the top fabric lines up exactly with that of the base, and then tack into place. Check again, and secure to the calico with fine herringbone stitches over the raw edge of the top fabric (*fig. 13*).

Release the tension slightly, and, working from behind, cut away the sheeting from behind the gauze. Retighten the frame, making sure once again that the warp and weft threads are at right angles to each other. This method will work equally well with a slate or a tambour frame.

It is vital for all embroidery, but particularly for the finer techniques in evenweave embroidery, to have a good light over the work. Daylight, obviously, is best, but if working in the evening be sure that the light is considerably better than one would accept as adequate for reading a book or newspaper. An anglepoise lamp, positioned so that it does not cast a shadow on your work, is ideal.

Transfer materials are not usually required for any type of evenweave embroidery, as all these techniques rely on counted thread to transfer the designs from charts. Resist the temptation to sketch directly on to the fabric with a pencil or with a dressmaker's or quilter's marking pen. Ordinary pencil marks are difficult to get rid of, and whilst the dressmaker's pen is supposed to make a mark which disappears instantly when touched with water, under some circumstances it has an unfortunate reaction with linen threads and leaves a nasty brown mark. If an outline is to be transferred, draw it out on tissue paper, pin this paper to the stretched fabric and then tack, with a contrasting colour, through paper and fabric, before tearing the paper away.

13

Having chosen the thread for a particular piece of embroidery, I like to make up a palette of colours. Taking a sturdy piece of cardboard (the back of a small writing or sketching pad will do very well), I punch holes in it around the edge with a leather punch, and thread through them the lengths of thread to be used. Each colour and make of thread is then marked beside the appropriate hank knotted through the hole, so that if I run out during the progress of the work I do not have to worry about matching the thread against a colour chart, or in a shop, but can reorder by number and name.

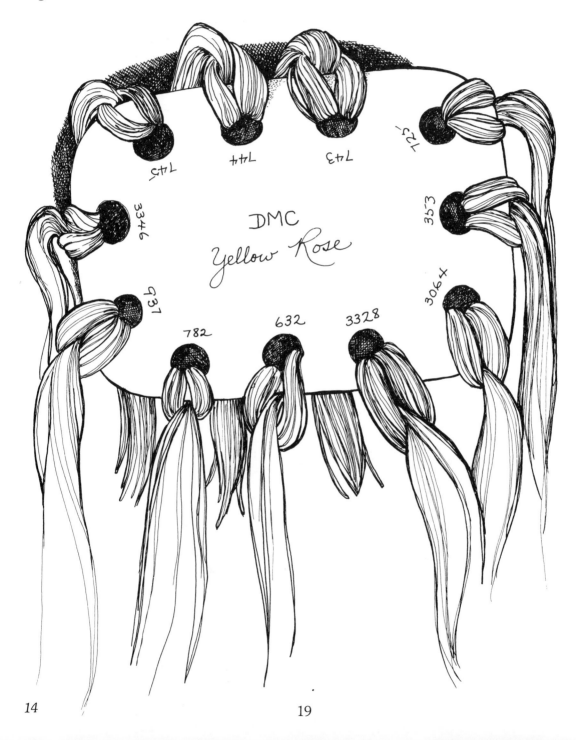

DMC
Yellow Rose

725
743
744
743
3346
353
937
306x
782   632   3328

This has the virtue, also, of keeping all the hanks of thread together without their becoming tangled. Skeins of coton à broder can be taken out of their papers and cut through, giving a useful working length of thread, but stranded cotton skeins, and skeins of crewel and tapestry wool, need to be undone carefully and wound around a large book or A4 pad to get a skein which, when cut in half and knotted through the holes in the palette, will give a useful working length.

Work in progress, when not in use, should always be wrapped in, or covered with (depending upon the frame you work on), sheeting or cambric, as otherwise the work will get grubby, especially if there are children or pets about.

I have not mentioned embroidery threads in any detail. In only a few cases will I suggest specific threads to be used in the different types of embroidery. Beginners will start with stranded cotton, but there are now so many different kinds of thread available, from fine lace threads to knitting and weaving wools, that it would not be possible to cover them all. In any event, half the fun of embroidery is experiment.

Further reading
Lady Marion Alford, *Needlework as Art*, Sampson Low & Co. (1886)
Mrs Archibald Christie, *Samplers and Stitches*, Batsford
Lynette de Denne, *Creative Needlecraft*, Octopus
Mary Thomas, *Mary Thomas's Embroidery Book*, Hodder & Stoughton

TWO

Cross stitch

15

Cross stitch is one of the oldest embroidery stitches, its first use probably occurring very shortly after the first cloth was woven. It is certainly one of the simplest stitches, and the most easily learned – witness its use for children's samplers in the eighteenth and nineteenth centuries. It is found, still, in peasant embroidery from India to Iceland, each ethnic group having its own library of designs and palette of colours. One rich source of cross stitch embroidery used to build up abstract or

21

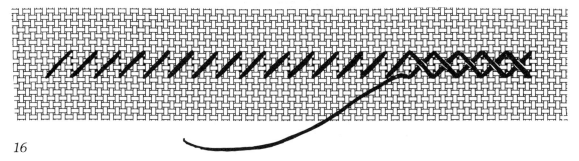

16

geometric patterns is found in the Slavonic countries, while people in western and northern Europe share an inclination to use the stitch to build up pictures which may cover the fabric completely, as well as to embroider patterns using the fabric as background.

Cross stitch is formed by working one diagonal stitch from bottom left to top right over a constant number of threads of evenweave fabric, then working back across the first stitch from top left to bottom right so that the two strokes thus formed cross at the centre on the front of the fabric.

Cross stitch may be worked one cross at a time, or by making a complete line of diagonal half

crosses from left to right, then working the return journey from right to left. (*fig. 16*).

Crosses are thus formed on the right side of the fabric, with vertical lines on the reverse. This method, where it is practical, tends to be more economical of thread than crosses worked singly, and is much more easily kept neat.

It is important to keep the second 'strokes' of the crosses all running in the same direction on your work (*fig. 17a*), as the light catches the irregularities and will spoil the effect if one is not careful (*fig. 17b*).

17

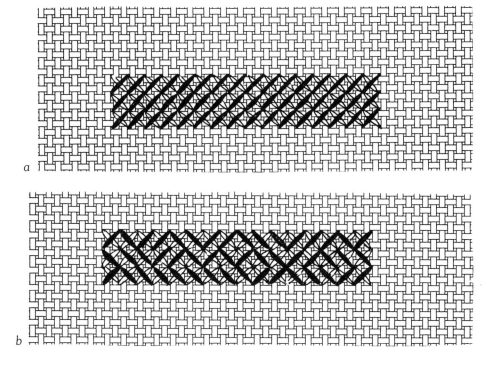

a

b

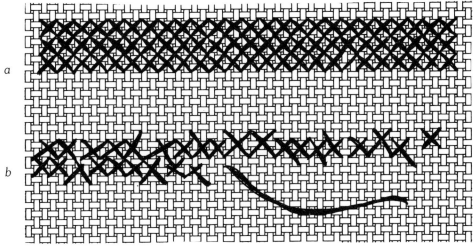

18

a

b

There are those who insist that there is a 'right' way for the top strokes to run, but so long as they all run the same way, I cannot see that one direction is preferable to another. Find the way which suits you best, and stick to it!

It is more important to ensure that the threads are counted carefully (*fig. 18a*) and the crosses worked over the same number each time, to avoid the result shown in *fig. 18b*. The thread used should be as near as possible to the weight and thickness of the threads of the linen. A heavier thread will give a chunky effect, whilst a thinner one will not cover the fabric but will give a lacy appearance. Both these effects can sometimes be desirable. Always try out the thread on a spare piece of the material before you start work in earnest.

Cross stitch can be worked to the same pattern on any evenweave fabric from fine linen to rug canvas, the design being enlarged or reduced by varying the thickness of the thread to suit the weight of threads of the fabric, and the number of

ground threads to the inch. A pattern can also be made larger or smaller by changing the number of threads worked over, remembering always to keep the stitch a square one (*fig. 19*).

Cross stitch is normally worked from a chart where each cross is represented by a square of graph paper. Usually this cross is worked over a block formed by two weft threads crossing two warp threads, but if you wish to enlarge the design it is quite in order to work over three, or even four threads (*fig. 20*).

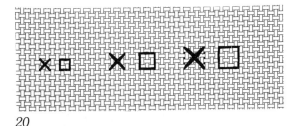

20

Needles should be blunt-pointed tapestry needles, which will slide between the threads of the fabric without piercing and splitting them, and should not be so large that they force the threads apart.

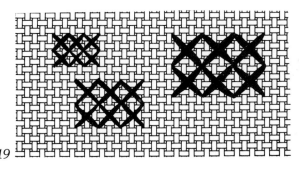

19

21

Cross stitch can be used in many different ways. In peasant embroidery it is found in many variations of spot and repeat patterns, varying from the very simple one in *fig. 21* to the elaborate vase of flowers found on an eighteenth-century German sampler (*fig. 22*).

22

24

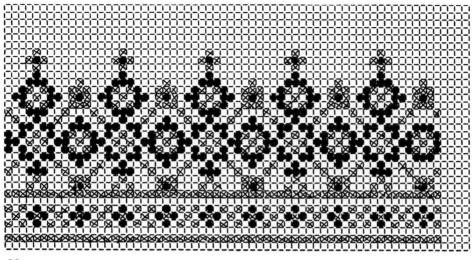

23

These motifs were frequently worked in one colour on white, whilst repeats and borders might be brightened by the use of a second colour, red and black being a favourite combination.

More realistic portrayals of animals and flowers were sometimes attempted. The deer in *fig. 24*, where the shape is outlined in cross stitch, comes from the earliest known dated British sampler, made by Jane Bostocke in 1598, which may be seen in the Victoria & Albert Museum in London. A

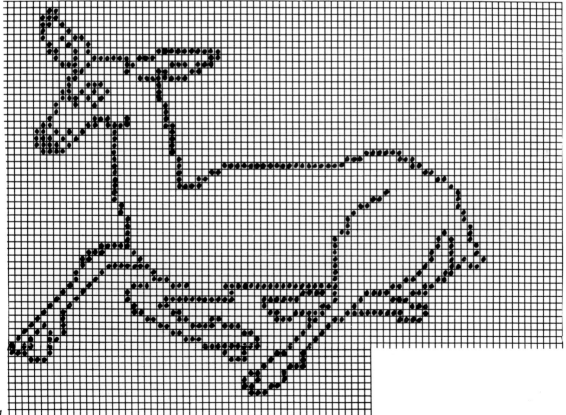

24

25

contemporary German sample book shows a deer in complete silhouette (*fig. 25*).

25

The roses in *fig. 26*, are a modern version of a traditional Russian pattern.

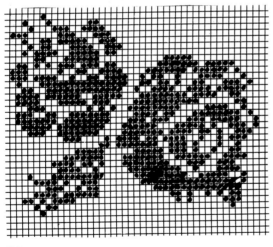

26

Difficulties arise when further colours are introduced, as different symbols are needed for each of the different colours.

Most commercial charts for cross stitch are printed in black and white, as the use of colour would make them prohibitively expensive. In a complicated pattern using several colours the jumble of symbols can be very confusing to follow (*fig. 29*), and it is sometimes helpful to colour in at least the major colour on the chart with watercolour before you start to work.

Should you wish to transform a sketch or photograph to cross stitch, there is a very easy way to do it.

Obtain a sheet of transparent graph paper of the required size (obtainable from some specialist stationers, or in booklets from some needlework shops). Lay this over your sketch, secure it carefully with drafting tape so that it will not slip, and with a pen, fill in the squares which correspond to the dark outlines of the sketch. You will find you have jagged lines instead of curves, and quite a lot of adjustment may be necessary to get a pleasing result (*figs. 27 and 28*).

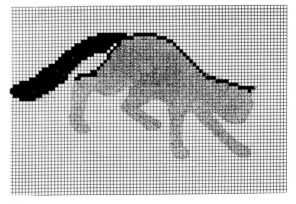

27

28

29   DMC colours (key)

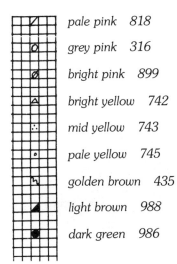

	pale pink	818
	grey pink	316
	bright pink	899
	bright yellow	742
	mid yellow	743
	pale yellow	745
	golden brown	435
	light brown	988
	dark green	986

Quite elaborate pieces can be designed and worked using this method. The dramatic face in *fig. 30* came from an advertisement in a Trinidad newspaper, while the original of the tiger (*fig. 31*) once made a plea for conservation.

A similar method is used for cross stitch patterns in colour. Felt-tipped pens or watercolour may be used, and it will certainly be necessary to simplify the gradation of colours when you translate the original painting to fabric and thread.

Two simple projects will illustrate the two main types of cross stitch.

31

Project 1: A small drawstring bag in 'peasant' cross stitch

Select a piece of white evenweave linen, 26 threads to 2.5 cm (1 in.). You will need at least a 30 cm (12 in.) square in order to mount it in a 20 cm (8 in.) tambour frame – the easiest way to work something of this size.

Fold your square in half and run a thread down the crease thus formed, following a thread of the material. Fold again the other way, and tack another line on this crease. Your piece of linen should now be divided into four. If the linen tends to fray at the edges, overcast them loosely.

Mount your fabric in the tambour frame so that the bottom left quarter can be easily worked.

Select your motif from those in *fig. 32.* Choose two colours of stranded cotton. These should go well together but be sufficiently different in intensity of colour to provide an adequate contrast.

Thread a No. 24 tapestry needle with two strands of the main colour, your thread being about 35 cm (14 in.) long. If you use a longer thread it will wear as it is pulled through the fabric time after time, and become fluffy by the time you reach the end.

You will need to position your motif so the edges are approximately 1.5 cm ($\frac{5}{8}$ in.) from your horizontal and vertical lines. Start by counting the squares on your chosen motif from the centre to the top. As there are two threads used in each square, double this number. Now add 16 (the number of threads to 1.5 cm) and count this number of threads down from the centre along the vertical tacked line. Mark with a pin.

Now count in from the vertical stitched line at this mark the same number of threads to arrive at the centre point of the motif.

Instead of knotting your thread, anchor it with a stitch near the edge of the tambour frame and run underneath the fabric to your first cross stitch. Knots form lumps, are untidy, and, on linen of this weight, tend to pull out.

Work the motif by counting the squares on the chart and transferring them to the fabric by making

32

crosses over two threads at a time. When you come to the end of the thread, or when it starts to become fuzzy from working, take the needle through to the back of the work and finish off by darning through the backs of the stitches. Undo the beginning of the thread and secure it in the same way.

New threads are now started by darning into the backs of the worked stitches.

At first you may have difficulty in counting the threads, especially when working diagonally, but with a little practice it becomes second nature. As most counted thread work depends upon the ability to count this way, the time will come when you will do it automatically – feel, rather than see, if you go wrong.

Remember to keep all the top strokes of the stitches running in the same direction. With some motifs the inclination is to turn the work in progress, and it is then very easy to make mistakes.

Once the motif is complete, prepare to make up the bag.

First of all, check that the furthest part of the motif on the right is the same distance from the vertical line as the furthest cross at the top of the motif is from the horizontal line. As you are going to pull out 10 threads above the horizontal stitched line any adjustment should be made there. Keep the pulled threads.

Fold the linen along the vertical line with the right side of the embroidery facing inward. Line up the edges of the pulled line, and pin securely. Using the pulled-out threads, backstitch the outline of the bag, keeping the stitches very carefully along the line of the grain on both sides of the bag (*fig. 33*).

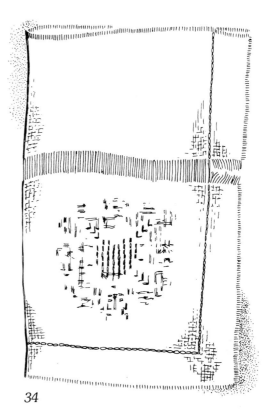

34

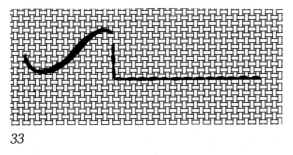

33

The stitched line should be exactly the same distance from the side and bottom of the motif as the motif is from the vertical guide line.

Extend the line of stitching (a new line) above the pulled threads (*fig. 34*).

Trim off the excess material above the pulled threads to leave a hem allowance of 6 cm (2½ in.). Trim the seam above the pulled threads to about 5 mm ($\frac{3}{16}$ in.). Fold in a small hem along the top, making sure that this fold is along the line of the threads of the material. Fold again so that the first fold lies along the top line of the pulled threads. Tack in place and hemstitch in bundles of two. (You will find this technique explained in Chapter 7.)

The extra threads of the pulled area should be cut and tucked into the hem.

Trim one side of the seam allowance around the bottom of the bag to 5 mm ($\frac{3}{16}$ in.), the other to 15 mm ($\frac{5}{8}$ in.). Fold the wider section over the smaller one, turning in a small hem, then stitching it to the

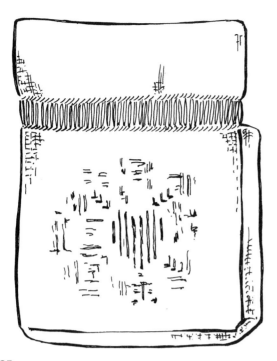

seam line. Make the seam very narrow on the corners (*fig. 35*). Turn the bag out.

You will need a cord for the drawstring. It may be difficult to find a ready-made cord which would go with the bag, but it is very easy to make a finger cord from the threads you have used for your embroidery.

35

36

Knot together two lengths of stranded cotton. For ease of explanation, *fig. 37* shows the cord worked with one dark and one light thread. Hold the threads in position as shown in (*a*).

37

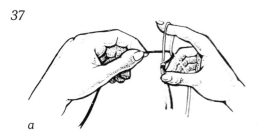

a

Still holding the dark thread firm, use the index finger of the left hand to hook the dark thread through the loop made by the light thread (*b*).

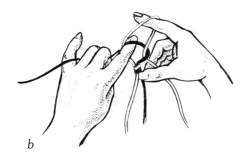

b

Pull the light thread tight (*c*). You will now have a dark loop held in the left hand.

c

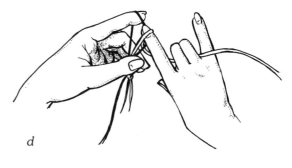

d

Using the index finger of the right hand, hook the light thread through the dark loop (*d*), and pull up the dark thread tight (*e*).

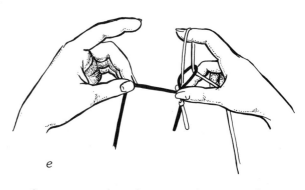

e

Continue working loops in alternate colours until a cord is formed (*fig. 38*).

38

It may be useful to experiment with stiff string until you get the knack of making a finger cord, but, once mastered, this is a very useful technique.

Using more of the embroidery thread, make two tassels for the ends of the cord.

39

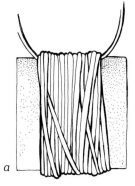

a

Wind the stranded cotton around a piece of cardboard cut to the size of the tassel desired (*fig. 39a*). Tie the strands tightly together at the top, leaving enough thread to tie the tassel securely to the cords. Snip through the bottom of the tassel (*b*).

b

c

Wrap a piece of embroidery cotton tightly around the strands a few times, tie securely, and 'lose' the ends inside the tassle. Trim the ends of the tassel (*c*).

Attach one tassel to the finished end of the cord. Thread the other end through the hemstitched line, weaving over and under the bands, and fasten the other tassel to that end.

These bags can be used as herb or lavender bags for drawers, or as containers for small gifts.

The more elaborate bag in *fig. 41* is worked on a much finer linen, 32 threads to 2.5 cm (1 in.), with a No. 26 tapestry needle, using the chart in *fig. 40*. It was made up in precisely the same way.

40

41

Project 2: Table napkin with red rose

For an illustration of the finished napkin, see colour pl. 3.

Take a 46 (18 in.) square of white linen, 28 threads to 2.5 cm (1 in.), and overcast the edges to prevent fraying whilst you work. (Do not hem it first – you will need the extra material to secure the linen in your tambour frame.) Draw out one thread on each side, 3 cm (1¼ in.) from the edge, to establish the corners and the position for your motif.

Work the motif charted in *fig. 42*, keeping the back of your work as neat as possible, since it will sometimes be visible.

Finish the napkin as set out in Chapter 7.

A companion design, for a yellow 'Peace' rose, can be worked from the chart in *fig. 29* (*see also colour pl. 3*).

●	986
◢	988
▼	902
S	816
H	321
∩	891
•	894

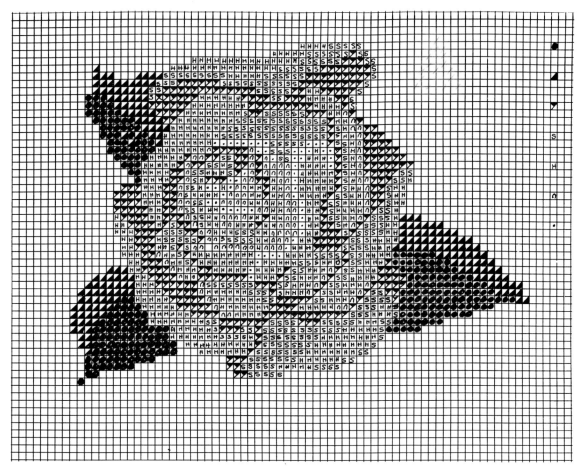

42 DMC colours

Two further types of cross stitch may be useful. The first is double-sided cross stitch, used where the pattern needs to be seen on both sides of the fabric. This is made by working down and back in each line twice, making extra half stitches at the right end each time (*fig. 43*).

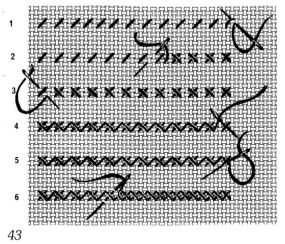

43

The second is 'marking cross stitch', which was much used for marking linen for the laundry, as it gave a very neat appearance on the right side of the article (*fig.44*).

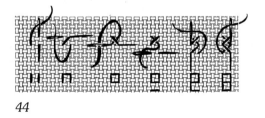

44

45

Cross stitch has always been much used for lettering. The two sets of alphabets in *fig. 45* come from a French pattern book published in the mid-nineteenth century.

46

Whilst no-one these days expects little girls of seven or eight years old to embroider 'improving' samplers in cross stitch, it is a happy thought to celebrate a new twig on the family tree with a traditional sampler (*fig.46*), or perhaps a 'name sampler' with lines of motifs starting with the initial letters of the name being celebrated, as in ' David' (*fig. 46*).

There are many more variations on cross stitch, but they will be dealt with in later chapters.

Occasionally one sees cross stitch which is very even but which obviously was not worked by counting the threads of evenweave fabric, as the crosses may be worked on any backing material from chiffon to leather. There are two ways these crosses may have been worked – first, from a transfer design, ironed on to the fabric, or, second, by tacking a fine scrim to the base fabric, and then working quite tightly, counting the threads on the scrim but stitching through both fabrics. When the embroidery is complete the threads of the scrim can be carefully pulled out, one by one, leaving the cross stitch on the tightly woven, or non-woven, fabric (*fig 48*).

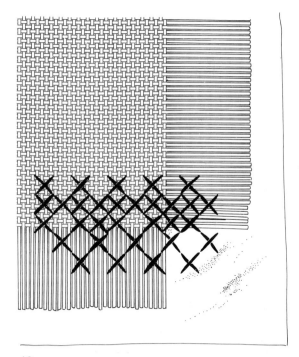

47　　　　Daisy
　　　　Anchor
　　　　Violet
　　　　Insect
　　　　Dog

48

It is fatally easy, when using several colours in a cross stitch picture, to get the thread count wrong when transferring from one patch of a colour to another patch of the same colour. There is nothing more annoying, when you come to fill in the intervening spaces, than to find you have left room for only half a cross (*fig.49*). It is possible to unpick cross stitch — but it is very tedious!

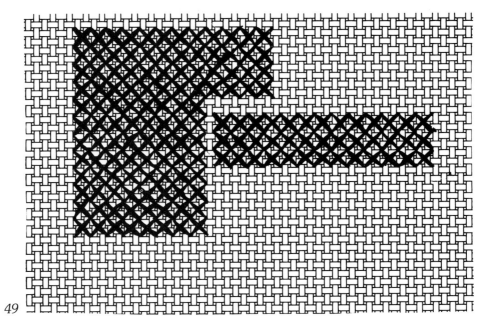

49

There is an easy way of avoiding this disaster. Work the first block in the first colour and then, instead of counting the intervening threads to the next block of that colour, work in the next colour, and continue till you reach the next block of your first colour. For instance, when working the chart in *fig.42*, start with colour 988, continue with 986, and work down with 902 and 321 until you come to 988 again.

Instead of finishing off each colour as you complete the patch, carry the thread to the back of your fabric and bring it out on the side of your frame nearest the work, where it is held until it is needed again, after the intervening colours have been worked. Try to ensure that this thread is not anchored at the back of the work by subsequent stitches in places where you don't want it held.

Further reading
Averil Colby, *Samplers*, Batsford
Marguerite Fawdry and Deborah Brown, *The Book of Samplers*, Lutterworth
Mary Gostelow, *The Cross Stitch Book*, Batsford
Needlework Alphabets and Designs, Dover Publications

THREE

Holbein stitch and Assisi work

Holbein stitch is so called because it appears, meticulously depicted, in many paintings by Hans Holbein the Younger, who painted at the court of Henry VIII. There is, however, no doubt that it was known in England much earlier, being fashionable in the time of Chaucer, judging by his lines from the Miller's Tale:

> Whit was hir smok, and browdid al before
> And eek bihyade on hir color aboute
> Of cole blak silk, withinne and eek withoute.

The possible implication of embroidery on both sides of the collar may well be that it was embroidered in Holbein stitch, or, more properly, double running stitch, which is the same on both sides of the fabric, allowing both sides to be seen to equal advantage. This made it especially useful on the ruffled cuffs and collars of the Tudor period, as well as on the elaborate hankerchiefs they carried.

Holbein or double running stitch should be worked on evenweave linen which is not so fine as to make the counting of threads difficult. The thread used should match those of the fabric in weight and thickness – too fine a thread will be lost, while too thick a thread will distort the pattern.

Whilst traditionally Holbein stitch is worked on white linen in black or red silk, any colour combination may be used so long as the contrast between fabric and thread is strong enough for the effect to be crisp.

The needle used is a tapestry needle of a size to suit the thread, and the fabric should be mounted in a frame.

As both sides of the fabric are going to be visible, no knots can be used when starting to work the pattern. Instead, it is best to start two or three stitches in from the edge of the design, work to the edge, overstitch the edge stitch, and then return over the original running stitches (*fig.50*).

50

Joins in the body of the work are achieved by cutting the finished thread off flush with the last stitch, and starting the new thread by repeating several stitches, being sure that no loose end appears on the work. This may result in a slightly thickened line, but is much less obvious than any other method (*fig. 51*).

51

To achieve a straight line which *looks* straight, work from left to right, over two threads and under two threads of the fabric, to the end of the row. Turn the work and fill in the spaces, bringing the needle out above the originally worked thread, and inserting it again below this thread for the next stitch (*fig. 52*).

52

This will give the appearance of a straight line, with regular, slightly slanting stitches, instead of the wobbly line which may result from less careful stitchery (*fig. 53*).

53

Very complicated designs can be produced with Holbein stitch, as the stitches may be worked

horizontally, vertically, or diagonally. When beginning, it is useful to work out the design on graph
paper first and plot the route of the stitches, as it is
easy to find oneself having to cross from one motif
to another or to leave empty spaces on one side of
the work, unless the outward and return trips of the
needle have been carefully planned.

54

a

Fig. 54a and *b* shows a method of plotting two
simple border designs for work in Holbein stitch,
while *fig. 55* shows a more complicated figure
where the return row of stitching would run along
the base line only.

b

55

Where the design is to be seen from one side
only, and is very complicated, backstitch may be
substituted for double running stitch in some parts
of the design.

Most of the examples of Holbein or double
running stitch which have survived from the
fifteenth and sixteenth centuries are on samplers.
Those shown in *fig. 56* were copied from small
motifs on an Italian sampler of the sixteenth
century in the Victoria & Albert Museum. They
could easily be used to ornament table linen today,
or even to embellish blouses or children's clothes.

Should you wish to make your own copies from
old embroideries (or from photographs of old
embroideries), you may find it useful, as I have
done, to use coloured (not black) thread on a fairly
coarse linen, and a felt-tipped pen on a large-grid
graph paper. I find it very difficult to copy the old

56

57

figures using pen and paper only, but intricacies of design often have to be sorted out on paper before you work them on fabric. Expect to make mistakes – and to find that the original embroiderers did, too. The coloured thread makes it easier to spot mistakes than black, which, for some reason, tends to mask them.

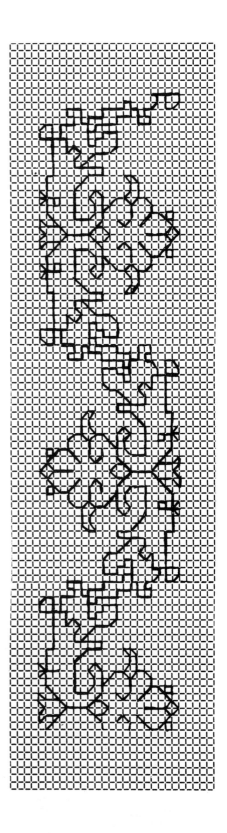

Once you have worked out your pattern, draw it out on graph paper (*fig. 57*). Examples taken from old samplers rarely have corners shown. If you wish to make a corner, experiment with a small hand mirror until you find a suitable one (*fig. 58*).

Those patterns which work strongly in one direction do not lend themselves so comfortably to this method (*fig. 59*). Instead, the pattern will have to be designed as a continuing one; if a mirror is used, a different treatment will be needed for alternate corners (*fig. 60*).

58

60

59

61

A curiosity which turns up again and again on sixteenth- and seventeenth-century samplers and on such embroidered linen as has survived, is the odd little pair of figures which twentieth-century collectors have named 'boxers'. It used to be believed that these were cupids or *amores*, and that they had come into English embroidery from Italian sources. In recent years, however, it has been accepted that these little nude figures started out as clothed lovers offering flowers to a maiden. Over the years, and via poorly drawn or embroidered samples copied by the not-too-skilful wielders of needles, whose work was in turn copied, the lovers lost their clothes and the maiden turned into an odd, two-footed flower – as shown in the sample worked from a border on an English sampler of 1749 belonging to the Victoria & Albert Museum (*fig. 61*).

62

Assisi embroidery

Whether or not Assisi embroidery originated in the little town of Assisi in Italy, it has certainly been worked there for centuries, first by the nuns on ecclesiastical linens, and then by nuns and lay workers alike on household articles and dress. Now the name of St Francis' home has become firmly attached to this type of embroidery, wherever it may be done.

Traditionally, the background of Assisi embroidery was worked in double-sided cross stitch (*see* *fig. 43*) in blue or rust, leaving the central figure voided. This motif was outlined with double running stitch, in black or another dark colour, sometimes a darker shade of the colour used for the cross stitch. The fabric most generally used was a very evenly woven linen in white or off-white. *Fig. 62* shows an Italian border in red silk, dating from the seventeenth century, at the Victoria & Albert Museum.

My attempt to chart this sample in *fig. 63* only served to convince me that seventeenth-century

63

64

Assisi work was much more elaborate than any-thing I have seen worked today. While I felt I captured the spirit of the piece, my version is much simplified.

When it is not important to view a piece of work from both sides, simple cross stitch, being much easier to work, has been substituted for double-sided cross stitch, and occasionally backstitch is used instead of Holbein stitch to outline the figure.

Although Assisi embroidery was traditionally worked with a background in one solid colour, there is no reason why this should be so today. *Fig. 64* below shows the chart for a 'Pig in a Wood', shown in colour in pl. 5.

65

Project 3: A small tablecloth in Assisi embroidery

Take a piece of pastel-coloured linen with a thread count of 28 threads to 2.5 cm (1 in.) 61 cm (24 in.) square. Select a colour of stranded cotton which will go with the ground colour to form a dark background in cross stitch. Select a second colour for the outline stitches.

Fold the square of linen in half and mark the centre line with a running stitch in a contrasting colour. Fold again the other way and mark the fold line with a second line of stitching along the grain.

The squares on the chart in *fig. 66* equal two threads or one cross stitch on the embroidery fabric, so the inside of the completed pattern is 386 threads across. Count down from the centre along one tacked line 193 threads, and start the embroidery at the centre point indicated by the arrow.

It is as well to work the top line of cross stitch all across the side before starting to work the cats in position, as this will give you a reference point. I find it best to work the central figure in full, then work the cross stitches between it and the next cat before outlining the second cat.

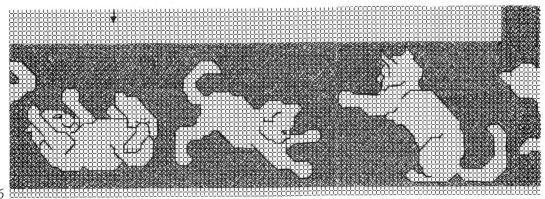

66

Because it is very easy to forget which way your cross stitch should run, work four or five half stitches above each side panel of embroidery to remind you. These may be removed later.

When the embroidery is complete, finish the edges of the cloth as shown in Chapter 6.

It would be possible to work a slightly larger cloth by moving the cats further apart, but too great a distance between them would spoil the effect. A cloth could equally well be worked using the pigs shown in Chapter 1.

Other voided embroideries

Other cultures have developed embroidery techniques where the main figure is voided, and the background filled in. The example in *fig. 67* is from

67

49

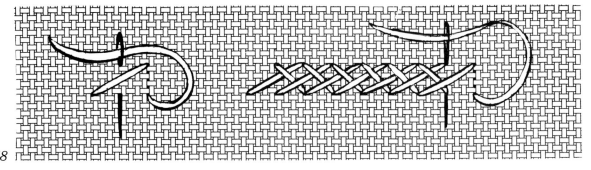

68

Morocco. Here the background stitch was long-armed cross stitch, shown in *fig. 68*.

Further reading
Pamela Miller Ness, *Assisi Embroidery*, Dover Publications

FOUR

Blackwork

Blackwork is any embroidery which is worked on white fabric with black thread. For our purpose, however, we can ignore those blackwork embroideries which are not worked on evenweave fabric and concentrate on those which are.

Holbein stitch is, of course, blackwork, and Assisi work can also be classified as such, but when we talk about blackwork today, we mean the complicated filling patterns which were popular in the sixteenth and seventeenth centuries and which have been rediscovered and developed by modern embroiderers.

For far too long I was convinced that blackwork embroidery was far too difficult for me to tackle. I had been experimenting with Holbein stitch and was under the impression that blackwork patterns were also supposed to be double-sided. The delight with which I discovered that this was not necessarily so spurred me on, and it was not long before blackwork became my favourite embroidery medium – and so it has remained.

Traditionally, blackwork was used as the flat filling of the shape of a leaf or flower, which was then heavily outlined with a variety of stitches in silk or metal thread (*fig. 69*).

When blackwork was revived early this century,

69

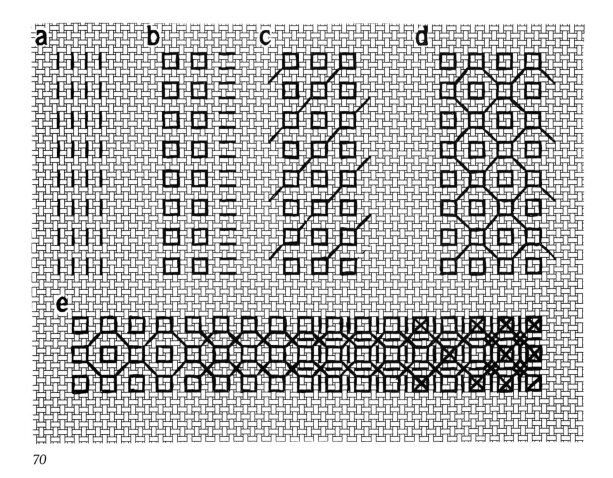

70

having been out of favour for over 200 years, the heavily bordered style was used again at first, but it was soon discovered how flexible a medium blackwork was, when used with imagination. While I have yet to see really successful attempts at incorporating a range of colour in experiments, I am sure there are few limits to the uses to which blackwork can be put.

A first attempt at blackwork should be worked with a black thread – DMC coton à broder 20, for instance, or two threads of stranded cotton – on a white evenweave fabric of not more than 26 threads to the inch. Do not attempt to work a picture as your first sampler – take time to learn the technique.

The fabric should be in a frame, as an even tension of stitches is vital for success. Anchor your thread with a knot on the surface of the fabric at least 5 cm (2 in.) from your starting point, and work a block of stitches over two threads and under two threads (*fig. 70a*) until you have covered an area of about 2.5 × 5 cm (1 × 2 in.). When this is complete, work at right angles to the first rows, joining the short lines into boxes by stitching over two threads of the fabric and under two, as before (*fig. 70b*).

Fig. 70c and *d* show these boxes joined diagonally, while *e* shows further developments possible with this grid.

Threads can be fastened off, and subsequent threads started, by catching into the back of the stitches. Make sure that the ends are anchored well, but do not allow them to stray across areas where there will be no embroidery, as they often make a shadow on the completed work where it is least desired.

Further stitches can be added to those in *fig. 70* which make it possible to add shading to a picture without using stitches which do not fit comfortably with each other (*see fig. 71*).

52

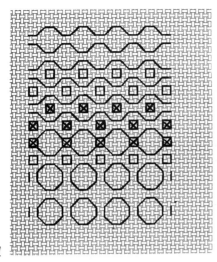

The chart in *fig. 72* was designed by a student of mine who intended to work it with this family of stitch patterns, the solid blacks being achieved with cross stitch.

The portrait head in *fig. 73* uses only this family of stitch patterns.

I have found no other family of patterns so extensive or so flexible. The three sets of stitch patterns shown in *fig. 74* illustrate how shading may be added.

72   *Cat by Kalpna Malkan, aged 15, Alperton High School.*

73

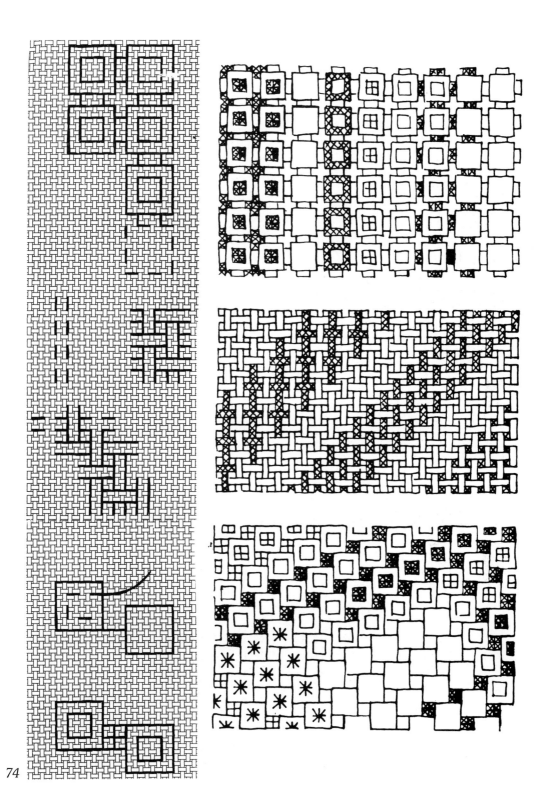

74

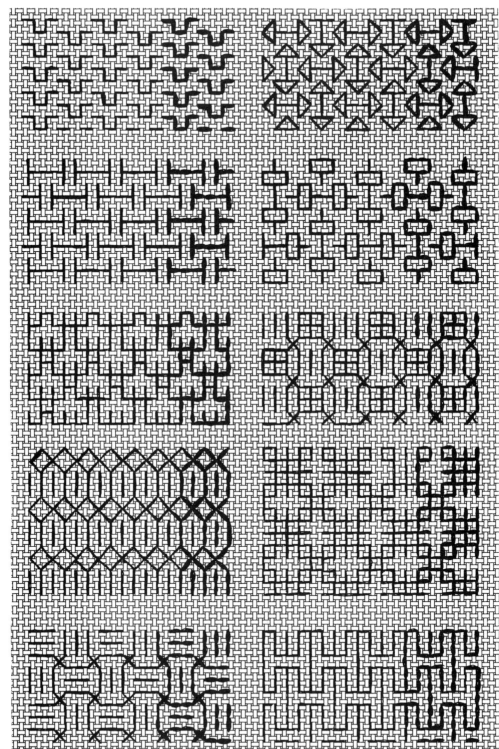

75

Stitch patterns such as those shown in *fig. 75* are fairly even in tone. Here shading can be achieved only by varying the weight of the thread used.

One quickly becomes aware that the drawn representation of the pattern can be very misleading when choosing stitches for an embroidery. It is essential to work a sampler in order to have on hand a reliable 'palette' of stitch patterns. It need not be so elaborate as the one shown in *fig. 76*, but needs to show a good range of patterns if it is to be of any real use to you.

Designing for blackwork

Every blackwork embroiderer has her own pet method of designing. I find two useful. The method I use depends upon the picture I want to paint with my needle.

Some years ago the Science Museum in London used Dürer's 'Rhinocerus' as a logo for their paper bags. It seemed to me to make a perfect subject for blackwork.

Taking transparent graph paper, I laid it over the drawing and traced the main outlines in red ink. The areas thus outlined were then filled in with blackwork patterns which seemed appropriate, and the outlines adjusted, where necessary, to suit the patterns (*fig. 78*).

The new outlines were traced on to tissue paper, which was tacked on to stretched linen. Red silk was used to tack along the lines, and the tissue was

77

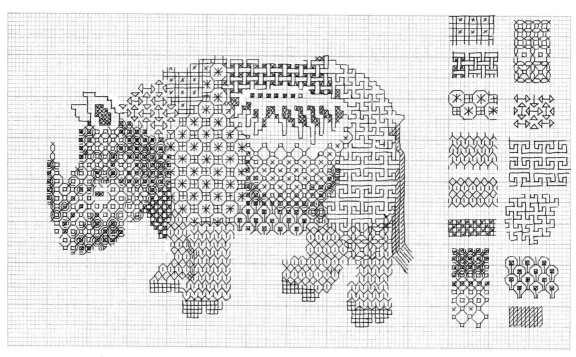

78

79

then torn away. The areas outlined were filled in with the patterns chosen and indicated on the master drawing. Because the squares on the graph paper did not coincide with the two-thread blocks on the linen, more of the pattern was used for each area than was indicated on the drawing, and a certain amount of adjustment was necessary as I went along. Some patterns didn't work too well visually when stitched, so others were substituted. The result is the rhino shown in *fig. 79*.

I feel sure, now, that the picture would have been more successful if it had been worked in a variety of weights of thread. One of my students worked the rhino from my original design and the result was quite different.

80

The head in *fig. 73* and the landscape in *fig. 80* were worked from pencil sketches, taken from life. In order to break the design for the head into areas of tone, layers of a simple dotted Letratone were used. This is a rather expensive method, but very effective – much more so than the use of varied weights of print from a newspaper, for when I tried this I seemed to spend all my time looking for the right weight of print.

81

The drawing of the cat in *fig. 81* has also been designed using Letratone layers. Adjustments would be made during working, but the broad areas have been established.

Over the years I have collected many blackwork patterns, some of which are shown in *fig. 82*. Most of these will be found worked on the sampler shown in *fig. 76*.

A

B

C

D

E

F

G

H

I

J

K

L

Whilst I was teaching children I found that the patterns in *fig. 83* quickly became favourites!

Any good book on blackwork will add to this collection, and it is always possible to find new patterns if you keep your eyes open – witness the design in *fig. 84*, from a brass floor vent in the Cathedral at Worms in South Germany, or that in *fig. 85*, from a plate purchased in the Souk at Rabat.

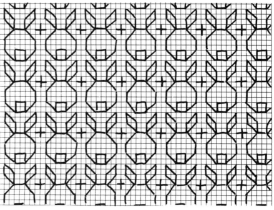

83

84

86

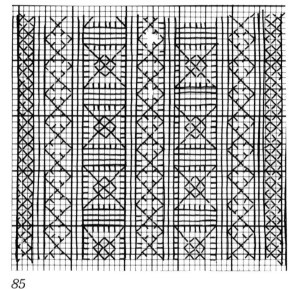

85

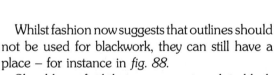

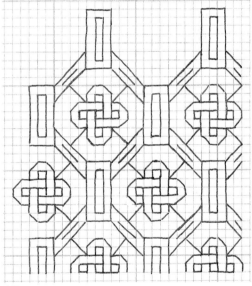

87

Whilst fashion now suggests that outlines should not be used for blackwork, they can still have a place – for instance in *fig. 88*.

Should you find that you cannot work in black on white with any degree of comfort, especially in artificial light, try working with a dark colour on a pastel shade, cream or grey. Often this is much easier on the eyes, and the effect can be charming. Or work on fabrics with a large weave – use knitting wool on hessian, for instance.

The remains of the mosaic floors of the Church of San Reparata in Florence (covered over when the Cathedral was built on the site, and recently rediscovered), provide designs laid out well before 1000 AD (*figs 86 and 87*).

88 'Footballers', by Stephen Anderson Currie.

Project 4: Greetings card

When I made the happy discovery that blackwork embroidery could be photocopied most effectively, a new way of making inexpensive greetings cards presented itself. Nowadays most people can avail themselves of the services of a photocopying firm in the local High Street, and should this firm have a photocopier which reduces the original by half, so much the better.

The card illustrated in *fig. 89* was worked from a pencil sketch.

An A4-sized outline was worked in red thread, on a stretched linen ground. The outlines of the sketch were traced and transferred, using tissue paper and coloured silk, as outlined in Chapter 1. The tissue paper was then pulled away.

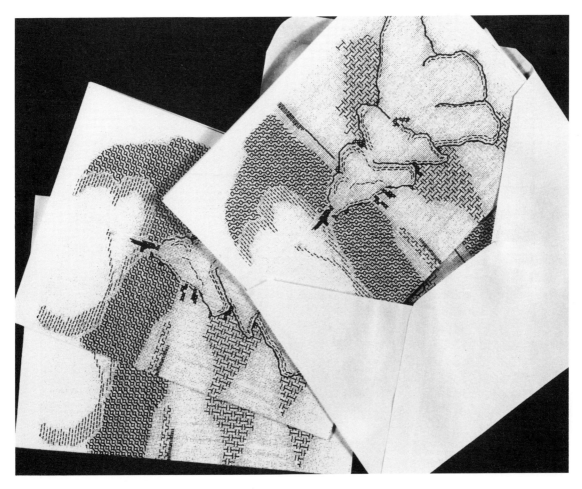

89

90

The picture was worked in black silk thread, using a variety of stitch patterns (*fig. 90*).

A greeting in cross stitch was worked on a second A4-sized panel. Both these embroideries were mounted and photocopied, reducing them to A5 size. These copies were then mounted as shown in *fig. 91*, and recopied, as many copies being taken as were thought necessary.

If the expense seemed justified, it would be quite possible to have the card printed by offset-lithography from this photocopy. In that case a stiffer card could be used, and the use of colour for print or background could be considered.

Further reading

Elizabeth Geddes and Moyra McNeill, *Blackwork Embroidery*, Mills & Boon
Mary Gostelow, *Blackwork*, Batsford
Margaret Pascoe, *Blackwork Embroidery*, Batsford

Peace
and
Goodwill

91

— FIVE —

Canvas work

Though often classified separately, canvas work is certainly a 'counted thread' embroidery. It is usually worked on stiffened, evenly woven material, made and marketed specially for the craft, though until comparatively recently (the last 150 years), canvas work stitches were worked on a linen scrim, or on any loosely woven evenweave material.

Even today canvas work is embroidered on a wide range of materials. The little picture shown in *fig. 92* was worked on silk gauze using fine silk sewing threads.

Here the only stitch used was tent stitch. This is a canvas work stitch for very fine work, used only on single canvas. It is usually worked diagonally, as shown in *fig. 93a* and *b*.

93

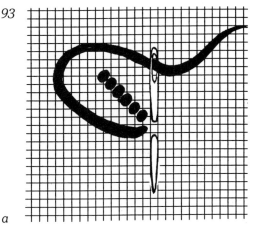

a

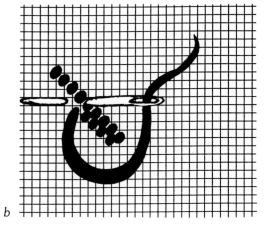

b

92

Worked in this manner, the fabric is less likely to be pulled out of shape, and a firm back is woven which gives a longer life to the embroidery than if it were worked horizontally (*fig. 94*).

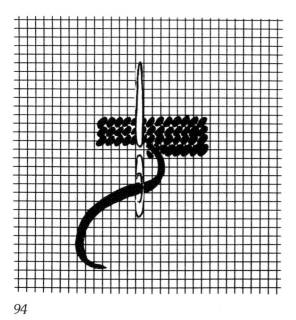

94

Where single lines or isolated patches of colour are to be worked, it is often necessary to use the horizontal method of working, but here the reverse of the work has only a row of vertical lines of thread, and it is more difficult to maintain an even tension.

Canvas work falls into three main types:

1 Pictures or hangings where the whole area of the embroidery is worked in tent stitch or cross stitch, the pattern being achieved solely by the variations in colour and tone of the silks or wools being used.

In the past this technique was used for wall hangings (to imitate woven tapestries) and particularly for upholstery. Today such embroideries are frequently worked by newcomers to embroidery, who are supplied – at a price – with a printed canvas and the wools to work it. Such kits are very useful to instil confidence in the timid, but most embroiderers will soon grow tired of covering large areas of canvas with one stitch, and will want to experiment with the textures supplied by other stitches.

Sometimes double canvas is used instead of the more usual single weave (*fig. 95*).

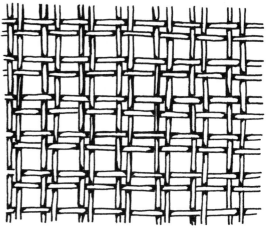

95

Where fine details are required (such as faces or flowers), the threads of the double canvas are forced apart and the details worked in tent stitch in silk or in a finer wool than that used for the background (*fig. 96*).

96

2 Patterned canvas work, variously referred to as florentine, bargello, flame stitch, or hungarian stitch. The origin of these names and their exact definition is the subject of much argument, but the embroideries are instantly recognizable, using as they do upright gobelin stitch in lines across the work (*figs 97 and 98*).

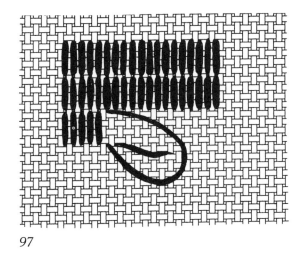

97

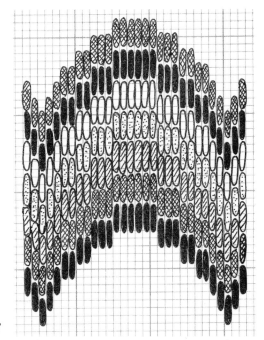

98

99

The cushion shown in *fig. 99* was worked by this method, using the chart given in *fig. 115*, which shows upright gobelin stitch worked over four threads, with a two-thread drop to vary the pattern. Whilst this is the most usual way of using gobelin stitch, a 4–1 drop is quite common (*see fig. 100*), as

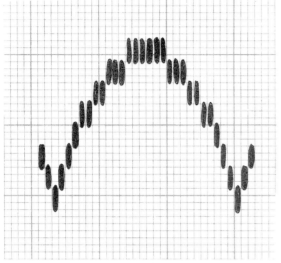

100

are 6–2 and 6–3 drops. Stitches over more than six threads are seldom practical, as they are liable to 'catch' in use.

Some florentine patterns are even more complicated. While they preserve the 4–2 drop, the lines of colour do not run in parallel lines across the work, but form patterns as shown in *figs 101* and *102.*

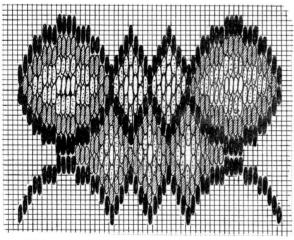

101

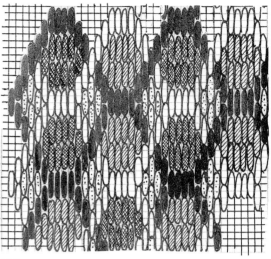

102

An even more complicated variation is hungarian point or 'flame stitch'. This is not to be confused with hungarian stitch (*fig. 103*), which is a canvas work stitch in its own right.

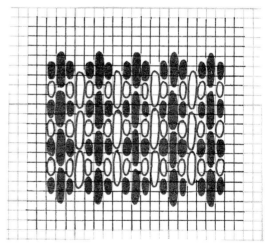

103

Hungarian point combines gobelin stitches over six threads with the same stitch over two to make a pattern (*fig. 104*).

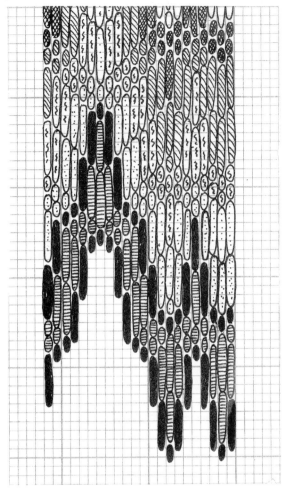

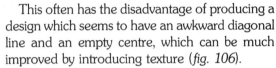

105

This often has the disadvantage of producing a design which seems to have an awkward diagonal line and an empty centre, which can be much improved by introducing texture (*fig. 106*).

106

104

By using the mirror technique from Chapter 3 it is possible to arrive at a design for florentine embroidery where the design is quartered – a very useful method for cushion covers (*fig. 105*).

3 Canvas work relying for effect on both colour and texture. There are several hundred stitches which can be used to good effect in canvas work, and it is not my intention to mention more than a few which I have found invaluable. Some provide a more interesting background (both to work and to look at) than tent stitch, some are tufted to give a velvet effect, and others are raised so that they provide shadows on the work which add greatly to the interest.

It is possible to use such textured stitches to make a background for free embroidery, as in the stitched and appliquéd peacock feather in *fig. 107*.

More usually, the stitches are combined with colour to build up a picture such as the cat in colour

107

pl. 10, or a pattern such as that based on crystal
forms on the cover of the jewellery case in colour
pl. 12.

One should build up a vocabulary of stitches so
that they come comfortably to mind when needed,
without prolonged thumbing through books.

Stitches can be catalogued as those worked diagonally (*fig. 108*), upright stitches, (*fig. 109*), stitches usually worked over four threads (*fig. 110*), which may include stitches from the other sets, and others, of which those in *fig. 111* represent only a few.

108

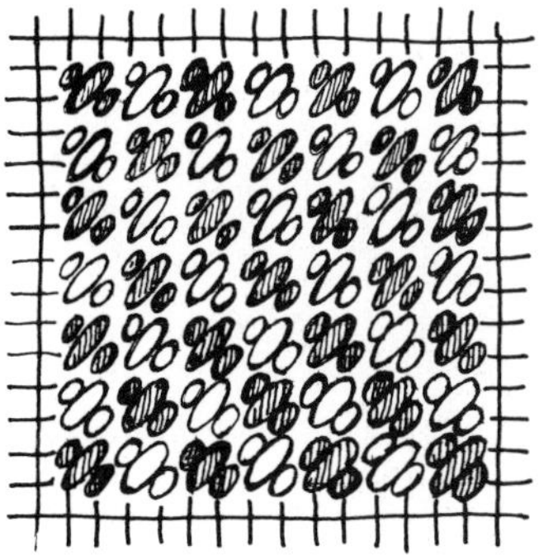

mosaic stitch

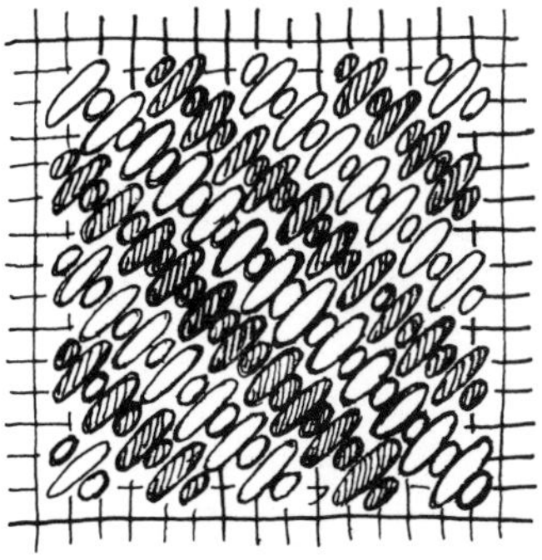

diagonal florentine stitch

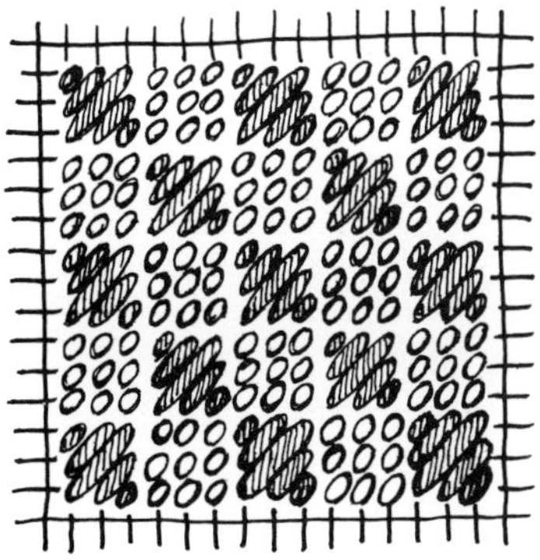

chequer stitch

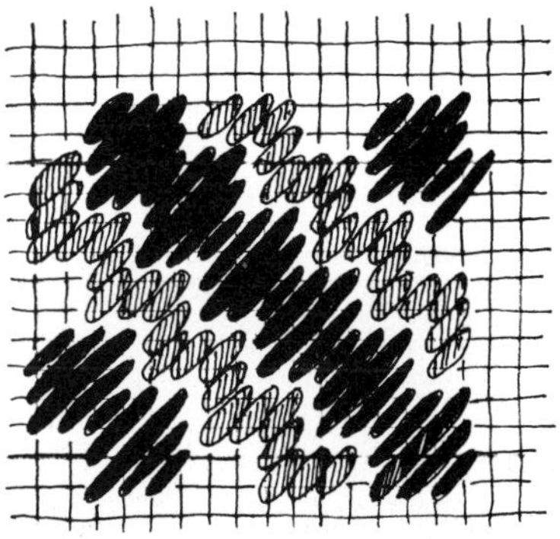

moorish stitch

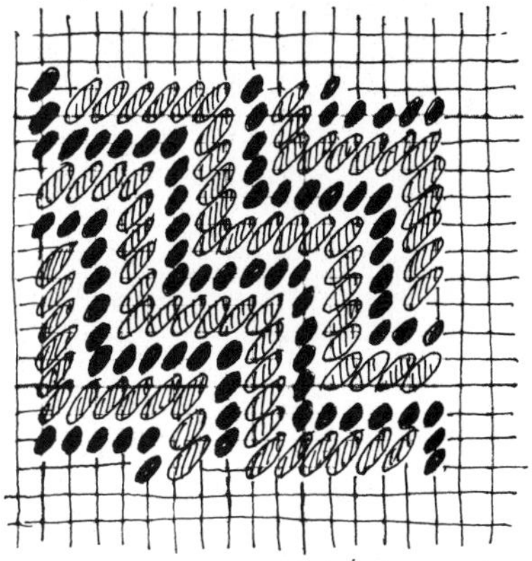

jacquard stitch

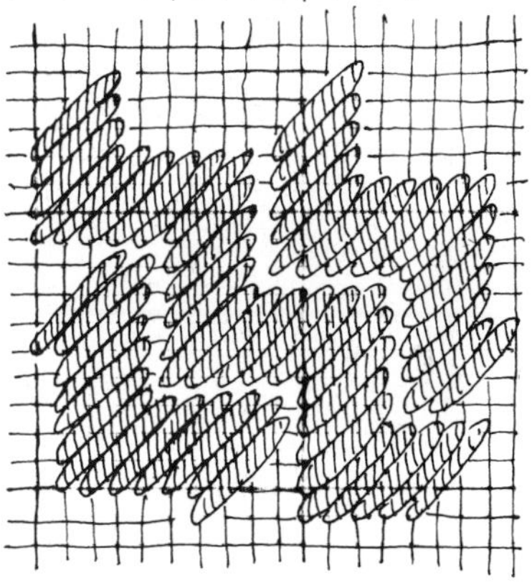

byzantine stitch

109

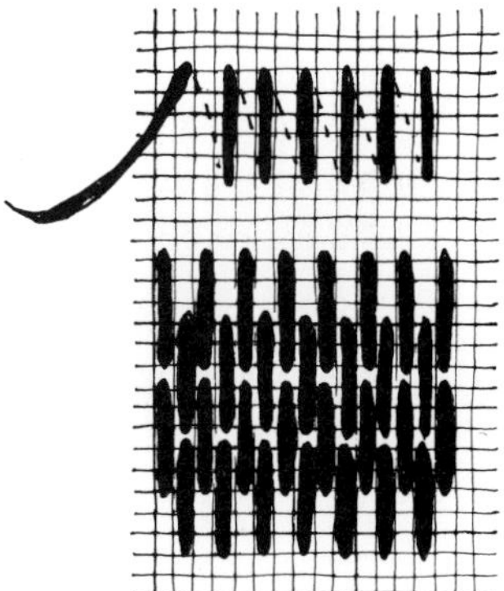

gobelin filling

75

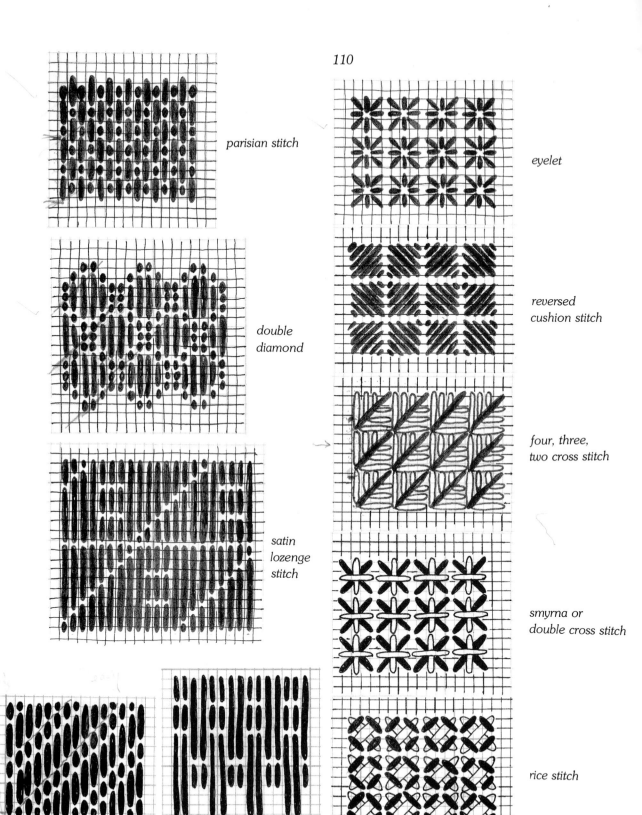

parisian stitch

eyelet

double diamond

reversed cushion stitch

four, three, two cross stitch

satin lozenge stitch

smyrna or double cross stitch

repp stitch

old parisian stitch

rice stitch

111

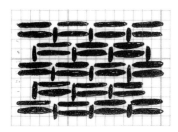

bricked filling

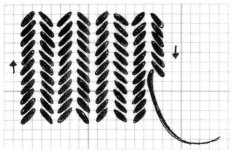

knitted stitch

leaf stitch

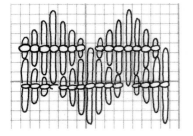

roman filling

satin triangles

'Sheila Flinn's Cat' (colour pl. 10) uses, besides tent stitch, variations on jacquard and scottish stitch and a pattern in bargello embroidery, satin stitch and rhodes stitch, as well as the fuzzy end to the tail in surrey stitch.

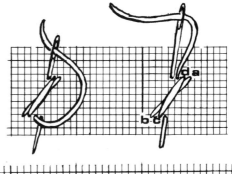

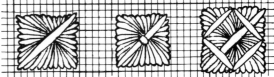

112   Rhodes stitch

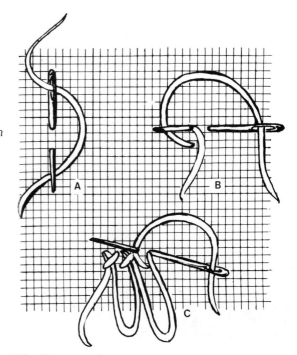

113   Surrey stitch

Project 5:
Florentine cushion cover

Choose a single-thread canvas with 18 threads to 2.5 cm (1 in.). Frame up a 50 cm (20 in.) square as shown in Chapter 1. This will allow a border of 5 cm (2 in.) all around the area to be embroidered. Stitch a centre line down this canvas in a fine, contrasting thread.

Choose a minimum of five skeins of wool. Preferably these should be in shades of two harmonizing colours, and should shade from a very dark colour to a very light or bright one.

Upright gobelin stitch does not cover the canvas very well, so it is important to use a wool thick enough to hide the canvas. For crewel wool, experiment with two and three strands before you start work.

If you are using a double thickness of wool, use one long thread rather than two short ones, which will wear out at the eye of the needle. Do not use a thread longer than 35 cm (14 in.).

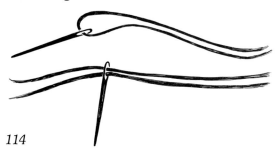

114

Using your darkest wool, start work at the centre line of the canvas. The highest point on the chart (*fig. 115*) is the centre of the repeat. Always work out from the centre when you start a piece of florentine work.

Make a knot in the end of your wool, and start the work by going in from the front of the canvas about 5 cm (2 in.) from the place you intend to start to embroider, leaving the knot on the surface of the work. Bring your thread up at the bottom of the first stitch. All stitches are over four threads and all stitches are vertical. The 'drop' is two threads in each case (*fig. 116*).

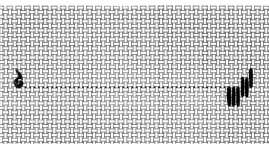

116

Work back towards your knot, covering and securing the thread behind the canvas. It will need several rows of the pattern to hold the wool in place before you can snip the knot from the surface of the canvas.

Following the chart, work to the edge of the cushion area. Should you have a length of thread left in your needle when you finish a row of a colour, you can carry it up the work, out of the way,

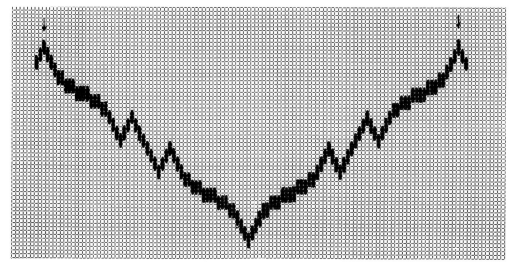

115

to be used in the next repeat. Finished threads are darned into the back of the work.

New threads may either be started with a knot, as for the first one, or darned into the back of the work.

Once the first row is complete, and you have checked that it is correct, the chart is needed only for the repeat of colours, which should be shaded from light to dark and back to light again.

Before long the lowest points of the lines of work will reach the bottom of the cushion area. If necessary, adjust the edge of the cushion shape so that the length of stitch used is either over the whole four threads, or a half stitch (two threads). Continue to work the pattern to a straight edge as shown in *fig. 117*.

117

When the square of embroidery is complete, take the canvas off the frame. Choose a backing fabric of corresponding weight – a sturdy furnishing fabric, for instance – and in a blending colour. Cut a piece of this fabric the width of the embroidery, plus seam allowance, and at least four inches longer. Off the end of this cut a piece about 12.5 cm (5 in.) wide. Fold over a small hem and machine a piece of Velcro (touch-and-close) fastening to the top of the fold.

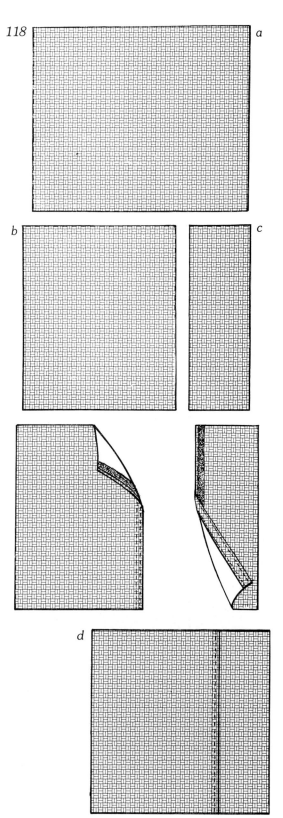

118

79

Fold a narrow hem on the corresponding edge of the larger piece and stitch the second side of the Velcro to the inside of the hem. Close the Velcro so that you have, in effect, one piece of material. Lay this face down on the right side of the embroidery and stitch the two pieces together, either by hand or by machine, making sure that your line of stitching lies right against the line of the embroidery stitches. Trim and oversew the seams, and turn right side out.

In the Bargello in Florence (the Museo Nazionale), there is a set of chairs covered in hungarian point embroidery (*fig. 119*). It is just possible that these chairs are responsible for the fact that the embroidery is sometimes called 'bargello', but no-one seems to be very sure. It might be nice to have a companion cushion, using the same colours as the first one, and the pattern from the Bargello chairs (*fig. 120*).

119

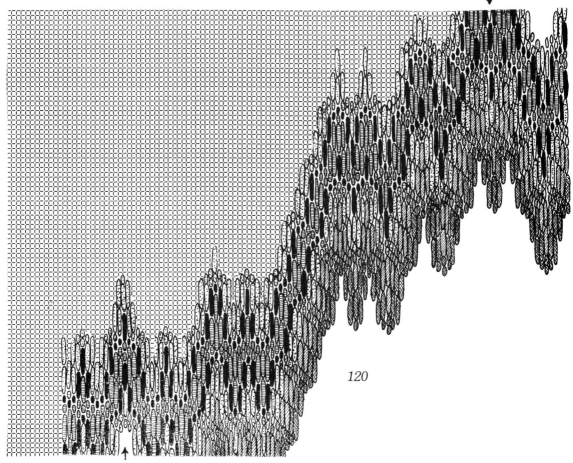

120

Project 6:
Canvas work pincushion

In the church of San Miniato al Monte, overlooking Florence, there is a black and white marble panel. I used the pattern as the basis for a large pincushion in canvas work (*fig. 121*).

Find the centre of the canvas and work a panel of cross stitches over four threads, 11 crosses each way, using the lightest blue wool. Using the wool, change the centre block of 5 × 5 cross stitches to rice stitch (*fig. 122*). Work the outside rows in rice stitch using the matching stranded cotton.

The rectangles around the centre square are worked in double cross or smyrna stitch (*fig. 123*).

123

On the rectangles touching the central square, the next darkest blue and the pink are used, wool on wool. The corner rectangles have the pink overcrossed with stranded cotton, with the darker blue for the outside triangle (*fig. 124*).

121

Frame up a suitable piece of canvas. I used a piece of double-thread canvas, 12 double threads to 2.5 cm (1 in.), because it was readily available, but single-thread canvas would do just as well. I used three shades of grey-blue crewel wool, and one of pink, as well as stranded cotton to match the lightest shade of blue and another skein to match the pink.

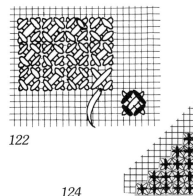

122

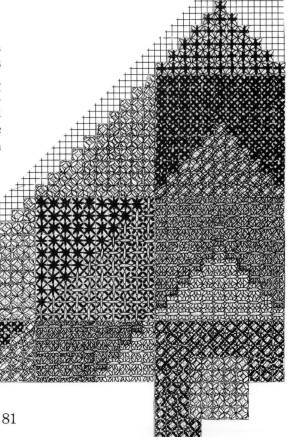

124

Rice stitch is worked again outside this rectangle, with the final triangles in the points in smyrna stitch again.

When the embroidery is complete, remove the canvas from the frame and trim off to five or six threads from the worked area, folding the edges under.

Place two adjacent corners together, and join the work along the line thus formed with long-armed cross stitch (*fig. 68*).

Continue joining the corners (*fig. 125*) and working the seams, until only one line remains open. Stuff the cushion with wadding, and work the final line.

It is not possible in one short chapter to touch on all the many stitches used in canvas work, let alone to discuss the use of beads, three-dimensional work, or of constructions using plastic 'canvas' or wire mesh. For those you must turn to specialist books, but the possibilities are almost limitless.

Further reading

The Coats Sewing Group, *Canvas Embroidery Patterns*

Diana Jones, *Patterns for Canvas Work*, Batsford

Mary Rhodes, *The Batsford Book of Canvas Work*, Batsford

Dictionary of Canvas Work Stitches, Batsford

Ideas for Canvas Work, Batsford

Diana Springall, *Canvas Embroidery*, Batsford

Elsa S. Williams, *Bargello, Florentine Canvas Work*, Van Nostrand Reinhold

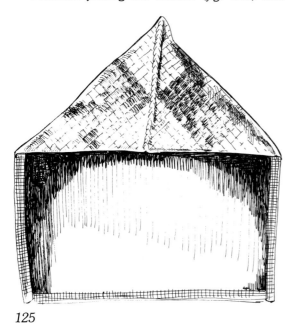

125

126

SIX

Drawn thread work

In the Victorian era drawn thread work (or withdrawn thread work) was used a great deal to transform evenly woven linen into a delicate, lacelike fabric, by drawing out sets of threads across the material, and working over those which remained.

Today the commonest use for the technique is in finishing hems in a decorative fashion. Should you never wish to use drawn thread work for any other purpose, you are sure to need to know how to prepare a rectangle of cloth for hemstitching, and how to work a neat hem.

Using a piece of evenweave linen, mark on it

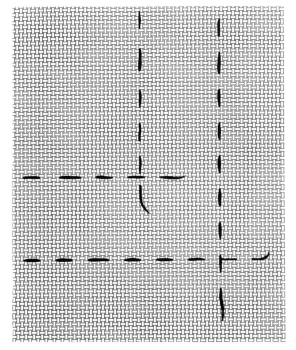

with running stitches in a contrasting colour the finished size of the cloth you require. You will need to allow a width of cloth all around this shape sufficient to give the required width of the hem (which should be the same all around the rectangle), plus turnings. The linen should be coarse enough in weave to allow the individual threads to be selected and pulled out easily.

On a first attempt it is useful to tack a second line of stitching all around the cloth on the line where the hemming stitches will be (*fig. 127*). This line should be a constant number of threads from the first tacking line all round. (The number of threads will depend on the depth of the hem required.)

Using linen with a count of 26 – 28 threads to 2.5 cm (1 in.), tack your guidelines, and then, starting about 15 threads from the inside corner, cut through 10 threads (working towards the centre of the cloth) and draw them out till they are about 15 threads from the next corner (*fig. 128*). Snip them

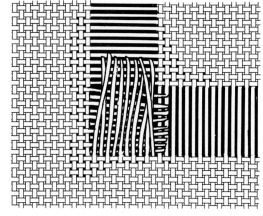

off. If the linen is of good quality it is worth while to keep these threads, wound around a spool, in order to work the hemstitching with them. This is especially important if a coloured linen is used, as it is often difficult to match the linen exactly with an embroidery thread.

Fold over the loose threads left at each corner on to what will be the wrong side of the work, and crease them firmly into position with finger and thumb. Using one of the threads pulled out of the work, stitch them firmly in place and trim off the ends. They will be hidden when the work is complete (*fig. 129*).

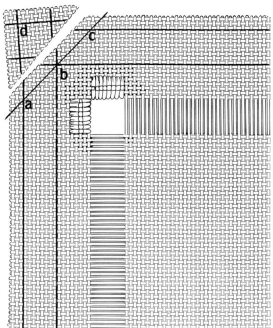

130

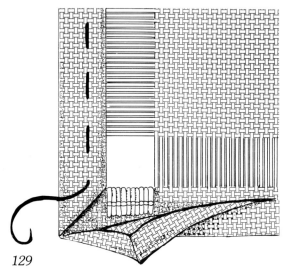

129

Fold the extra material allowed along the outer tacked line. Make a second fold so that it lies along the edge of the drawn out threads. Fold firmly along these lines so that the crease is visible when the material is opened out again. Do this all this way around the cloth and open out. The tacked lines of the edge of the finished cloth will cross at *d* in *fig. 130*. The creased lines of the edge of the fold will cross at *b*.

The corner of the cloth is now folded over so that point *d* rests on the corner of the drawn out area, and the crease now folded falls on *b*, cutting the creased lines of the folded edges at *a* and *c*.

Open out and cut the corner off, leaving enough material to ensure a secure seam.

Fold the cloth diagonally so that line *ab* lies along line *bc*. Thread a needle with some more of the thread drawn from the fabric, and backstitch

along this line very firmly, finishing at point *ac*. Should you feel nervous, cut the corner off *after* the seam has been backstitched, so that you can check it is correct (*fig. 131*).

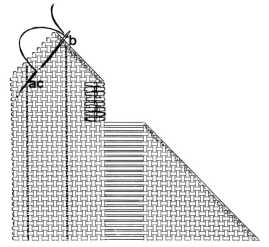

131

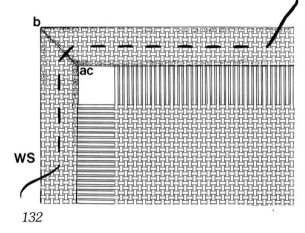

132

The backstitched seam is now pressed open, and the corner turned out. Fold the allowance under, and tack the hem in position. On the wrong side it should look like *fig. 132*, and on the right side of the cloth like *fig. 133*.

Mitreing a corner is a process which seems to fill even experienced embroiderers with terror, but done methodically, it is really very simple.

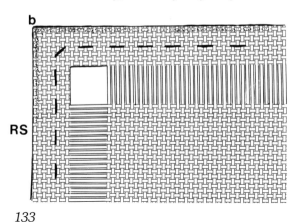

133

Working on the wrong side of the cloth, proceed to hemstitch the hem in place, as shown. The thread, which again can be one drawn from the fabric, is secured between the folds of the hem, and the stitch worked as shown in *fig. 134*. For simple

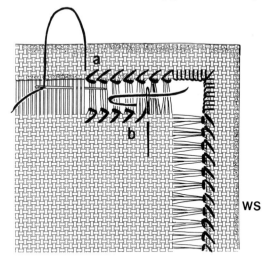

134

ladder hemstitch it is sufficient to gather three threads into each bunch. Corners are secured with buttonhole stitch (*fig. 135*).

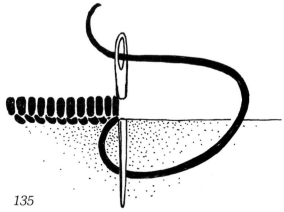

135

Unless you have been very careful – or very lucky – you will find you are left with an extra thread at the end of the row, when you come to turn the corner. This miscalculation will be much less obvious if you make the adjustment several stitches back. In *fig. 136* the work is being done with groups of two threads.

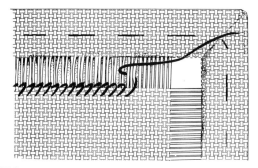

136

By using groups of four, it is possible to split these clusters on the second side of the hemstitching, and arrive at a zig-zag pattern (*fig. 137*).

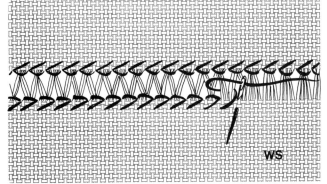

137

There are many methods of decorating the area of drawn threads. One simple way is to anchor an embroidery thread (not the drawn out fabric thread this time, as it will not be long or strong enough) at the corner of the cloth, and then to twist the clusters with the needle as you take the thread across the work to anchor it on the other side (*fig. 138*). Or

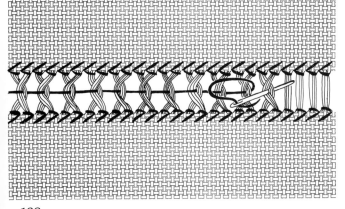

138

anchor a thread at the corner and then knot together series of three clusters of ladders all across the work (*fig. 139*).

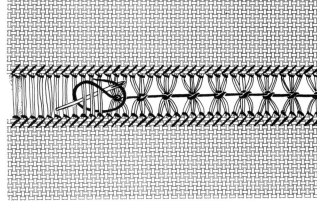

139

Any of these methods of finishing a hem will leave a very plain corner. Some decoration is obviously desirable. A favourite method with the Victorians was the whipped spider's web (*fig. 140*).

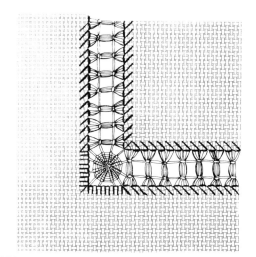

140

Here, two rows of thread knot the bunches of ladders together and are anchored at the corner.

Additional threads are laid from corner to corner of the open space, and then a whipped spider's web is worked over the threads which have been caught together in the centre. To get to the centre it will be necessary to whip the thread over one of the spokes, but this will not show (*fig. 141*).

141

142

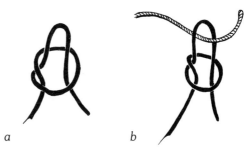

a   *b*

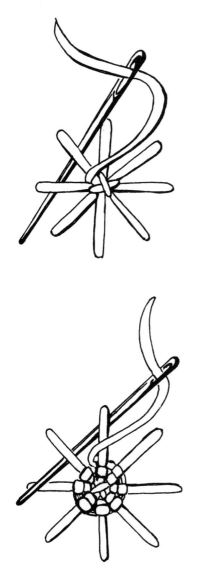

A slip knot is made in the end of one thread (*fig. 142a*), and the end of the other thread inserted into it (*b*). The first thread is pulled up very tight, so that it clicks (*c* and *d*). Tug the two threads to make sure that the knot is firm, (*e*) and then cut off close to the knot before proceeding.

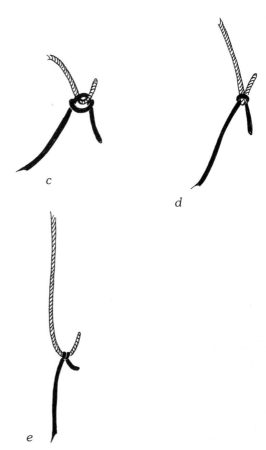

c

d

e

When working these decorations one should aim to use a long enough thread, so that no joins are necessary. This is not always possible, and when a join cannot be avoided, a lace knot can be used.

This knot is only to be used in places where the thread is not required to be pulled through the fabric.

The handkerchief shown in *fig. 143* has, besides decoration in simple ladder hemstitch, an interesting elaboration of the design in *fig. 139*. A tiny spider's web in the centre of a knotted circle, is surrounded by even smaller webs, and a row of knots.

A second handkerchief, in *fig. 144*, relies almost entirely on drawing and buttonholing, with only a little extra thread introduced.

143

144

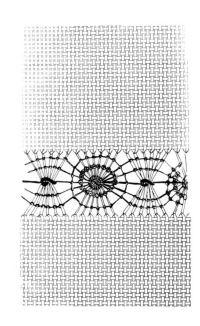

145

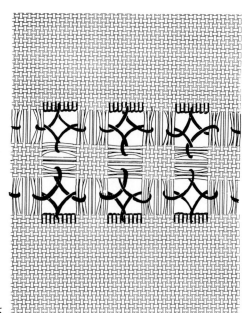

146

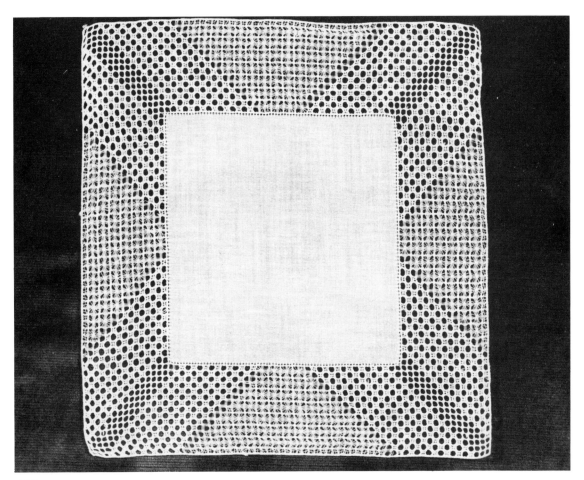

147

The handkerchief shown in *fig. 147* (a souvenir of a trip to Spain many years ago) has a wide border of drawn thread worked with a thread only a little stronger and thicker than those of the fabric.

In general, threads used for drawn thread work should be of the same weight and colour as those of the ground fabric. Lace threads, coton perlé and coton à broder will all find their place. Another simple decoration useful for a beginner to know is Italian hemstitch, where two sets of threads are drawn out. The outside rows are worked normally, but the centre bar of woven fabric is worked as shown in *fig. 148*.

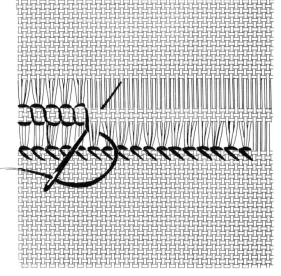

148

It is a logical progression to go from simple hemstitching and its variations to needleweaving, a very simple form of which is shown in *fig. 149*.

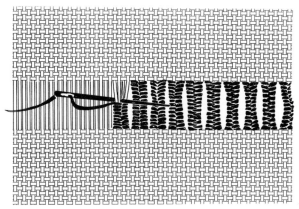

149

150

Fig. 150 shows a sampler mat, with four needlewoven borders, and four corners embellished with needleweaving. One border has already been shown. Opposite it is an elaboration of the first, where the needleweaving is done over four threads, but halfway up the space two threads are dropped and the two adjacent threads woven in. This means that the needle must be slipped back to the join through the back of the stitches already worked (*fig. 151*).

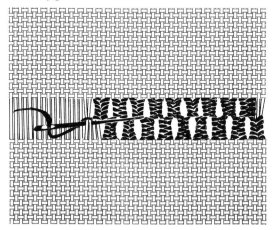

151

The third side is worked with pyramids of needleweaving. It is best to establish the centre of the row to be worked, and start there, as otherwise it is almost inevitable that the design will be unbalanced. Work over two threads or clusters of threads, adding in steps at each side until there are ten threads being worked over (*fig. 152*). Try to keep the steps even. It may even be worth while marking the lines across the loose threads as a guide.

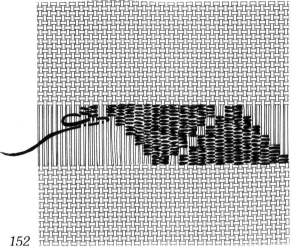

152

The fourth side is worked in stepped groups again, but the effect is quite different, as so much more of the basic thread is left unworked – although, as shown in *fig. 153*, it is possible to whip these unwoven threads.

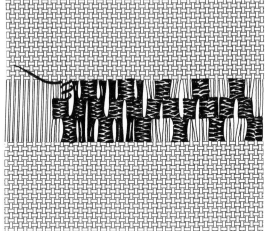

153

The first corner is worked by taking two threads horizontally and vertically across the open space, and then diagonally as well. A whipped spider's web is worked over the centre, and then the double threads are needlewoven (*fig. 154*).

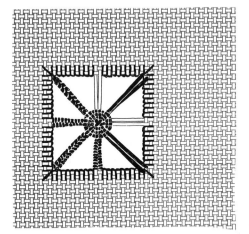

154

The second corner has three threads laid across, horizontally and vertically, and then on both diagonals. They are caught at the centre and then all the sets of three threads are needlewoven (*fig. 156*).

155

The third corner has single horizontal and vertical threads, diagonal threads, and then further diagonal threads added, these being woven into a shamrock shape as shown in *fig. 156*.

156

The fourth corner employs the method used in *fig. 140*.

Other forms of embroidery on evenweave fabric need to be worked in a frame, but many people find it easier to work hemstitching and needle-weaving in the hand. So long as the tension is kept even, there is no reason why this should not be successful.

Project 7: Small cloth in drawn thread work

A piece of good-quality linen, approximately 30 threads to 2.5 cm (1 in.) is required. This should measure at least 50 × 40 cm (20 × 16 in.).

Fold to find the centre, and tack centre lines in contrasting thread, vertically and horizontally, along the grain lines. Count 70 threads from the centre along one of the short tacked lines. Cut through 10 threads. Count 20 threads and then cut through 10 more. Draw out these two sets of 10 threads to left and right of the centre line for at least 50 threads to each side.

You will have a band of drawn threads, a band of solid weave 20 threads wide, and another band where 10 threads have been drawn.

Count 10 threads to either side of the contrasting tacked line and cut through 10 threads on either side of the woven band. Draw out these 10 threads, leaving ends at each outside edge which will later be fastened off. You will have a woven square, 20 threads each way, with a band around it where 10 threads have been drawn out either side, top and bottom (*fig. 158*).

Continue to work either side of the central line until you have 11 woven squares along one side. Work seven squares (including the end square of your first row) at right angles, and continue around the cloth until you have outlined all 32 squares with bands of drawn threads.

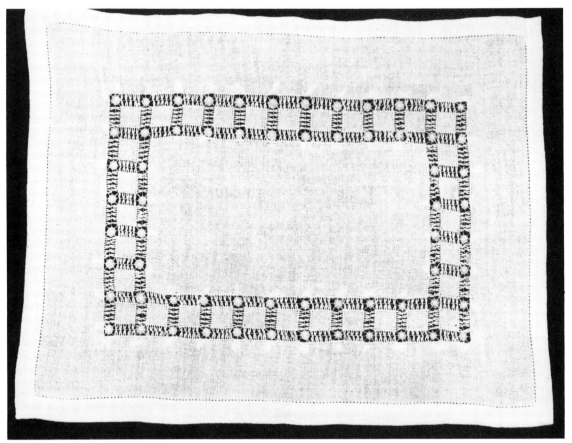

157

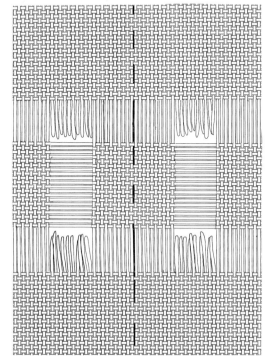

Clip off the long threads you have withdrawn, leaving enough to turn over to the wrong side of the work and stitch down (*see fig. 129*). Now work the drawn areas, buttonholing where the threads leave a raw edge, and hemstitching the loose threads remaining into ladders, using bunches of two threads. Hemstitch around the squares (*fig. 159*).

158

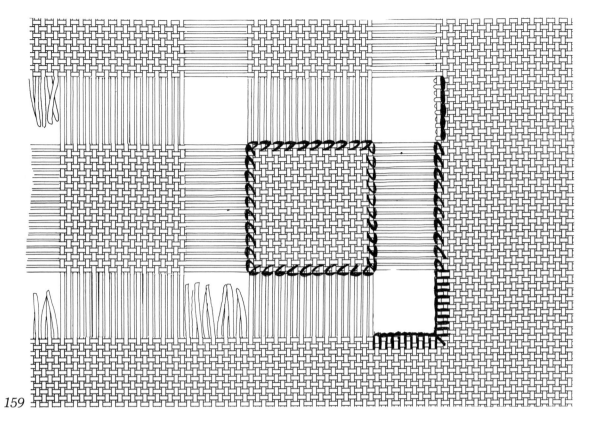

159

Using coton perlé No. 20 in a colour to match the fabric, and a No. 26 tapestry needle, anchor the thread in the buttonhole stitch on the inside edge of the pattern, carry it across the ladders, bunching them into groups of two with a coral knot (*fig. 160*), and secure it on the outside edge. Continue till all the short runs are complete (*fig. 161*).

Take a long thread in your needle, anchor the thread at one corner, and work to the next, bunching the ladders as before.

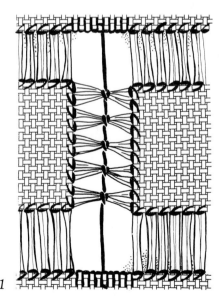

160

161

When all the open spaces have been crossed, work a corner. There is already a vertical and a horizontal thread at the corner. Put in two diagonals, carry the thread to the centre and work a spider's web which nearly fills the space (*fig. 162*). Fasten off. Do the same in all the other spaces (64 spiders!).

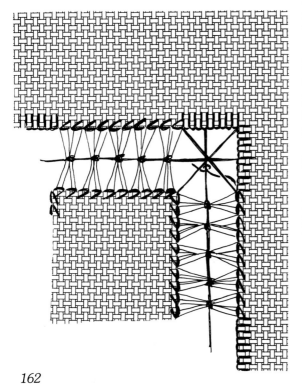

162

When all the embroidery has been worked, measure out 4.5 cm (1¾ in.) from the outer line of the embroidery and draw out one thread on each side until they meet at the four corners. Cut off. Trim each edge to 3 cm (1¼ in.) from the drawn thread, making sure that you cut on a thread line. Fold over a raw edge of 0.5 cm (¼ in.) and place this fold to the drawn line. Crease. Work the hem and mitred corners as shown earlier in this chapter. Your hemstitch will fill the drawn line.

Drawn thread work is quite sturdy and can be laundered with only a little more care than you would give a piece with surface embroidery. When pressing, place the embroidery face down on towelling so that the spider's webs are not flattened.

Further reading
The Anchor Manual of Needlecraft, Batsford
DMC Library, *Drawn Thread Work*
Mary Thomas, *Mary Thomas's Embroidery Book*, Hodder & Stoughton

1 Tiger worked in cross stitch, using a design taken from a conservation poster *(see Chapter 2).*

2 Small drawstring bag in 'peasant' cross stitch *(see Chapter 2).*

3 *(Below)* Table napkins with red and yellow rose motifs in cross stitch *(see Chapter 2).*

4 *(Opposite)* A traditional-style cross stitch sampler designed to celebrate a special event *(see Chapter 2).*

5 *(Top left)* 'Pig in a Wood'. A modern version of Assisi stitch, with the background worked in several different colours *(see Chapter 3)*.

6 *(Left)* Rhinocerus in blackwork, taken from an engraving by Dürer *(see Chapter 4)*.

7 *(Above)* Blackwork sampler, showing a wide range of stitch patterns *(see Chapter 4)*.

8 Cushion cover in florentine work on single-thread canvas *(see Chapter 5)*.

9 Cushion cover using a pattern taken from a chair cover in the Bargello *(see Chapter 5)*.

10 'Sheila Flinn's Cat'. Picture incorporating tent stitch, variations on jacquard and Scottish stitch, bargello, satin stitch, rhodes stitch and surrey stitch *(see Chapter 5)*.

11 Panel based on fungus, using florentine embroidery, canvas work stitches and raised chain band, with padded appliqué in leather, plastic, and fabric *(see Chapter 10).*

12 Jewellery case using a design based on crystal forms, in canvas work stitches using a variety of threads, as well as leather appliqué *(see Chapters 5 and 10).*

SEVEN

Drawn fabric embroidery

In this type of embroidery the threads are not withdrawn from the fabric, the lacy effect being achieved by working suitable stitches tightly in a strong linen or cotton thread so that the threads of the fabric can be drawn or pulled out of place to form an openwork pattern. This embroidery is much stronger than drawn thread work as the threads are not removed from the fabric but merely displaced. It is sometimes referred to as pulled thread work.

The work should be done on evenweave linen or on a fine linen scrim, where the threads can be counted easily. In the past muslin and voile were used for dress embroidery, but this is very painstaking work, and not advised for the beginner – or for anyone who values their eyesight.

Traditionally, the shapes were worked in a variety of stitches, and outlined with either a line of some raised stitch, or with petals and leaves in padded satin stitch. Modern pulled work is more often worked without such outlines, the stitches themselves forming the shapes.

The stitches are worked in a strong thread, linen being the most successful, though coton à broder and coton perlé can be used, together with finer lace threads where their use is applicable. The thread should be slightly finer than the background fabric, and match it exactly in colour.

A tapestry needle which will comfortably take the thread is used. Even on fine work a No. 26 is often too fine, as the eye will sometimes collapse when pulled hard.

Charts for drawn fabric stitches are confusing, since the chart bears very little resemblance to the

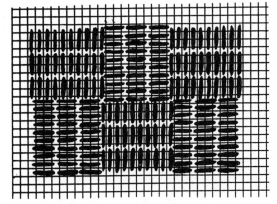

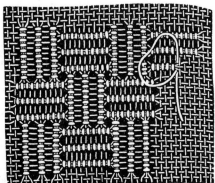

163

finished stitch. As an illustration, *fig. 163* shows a chart for basketwork stitch beside a drawing of the worked stitch.

It is essential to work a sampler of drawn fabric stitches before you start to work in earnest, as there is no other way to learn what they will really look like when finished.

The cityscape in *fig. 164* was my first effort at drawn fabric, worked many years ago, but it is still useful as a sampler. Compare the worked stitches

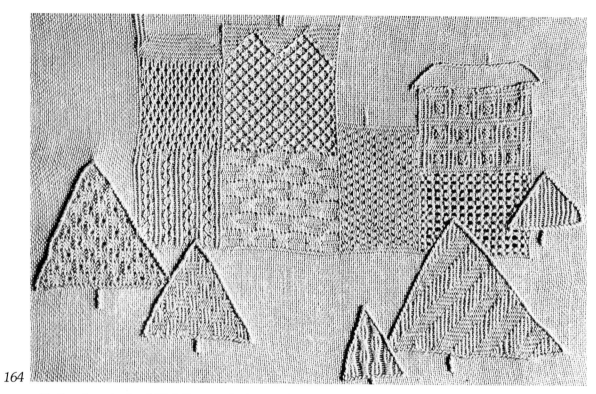

164

with the chart in *fig. 165*, following the key in *fig. 166*, and you will see how misleading charts can be for choosing a stitch.

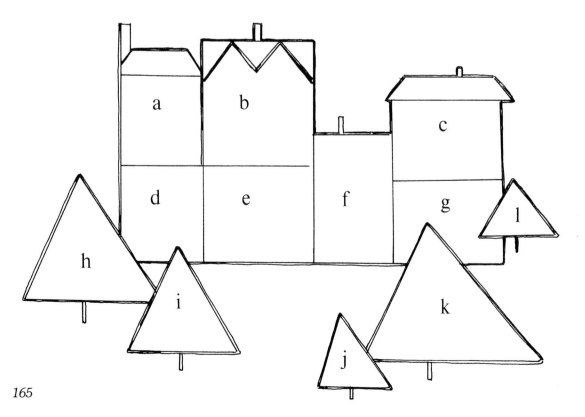

165

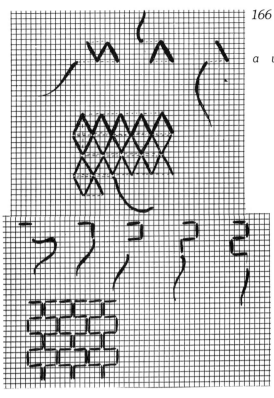

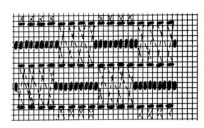

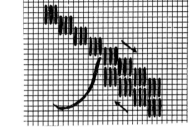

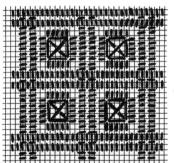

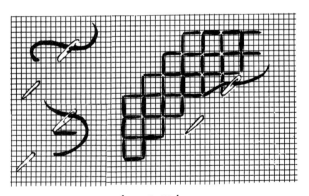

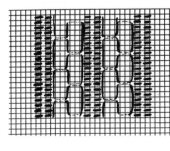

166

a   wave stitch

b   honeycomb
filling

c   Maltese filling

d   cording
and honeycomb

e   cording
and backstitch

f   Algerian filling

g   faggot stitch

99

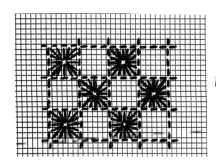

h backstitched
   eyelet

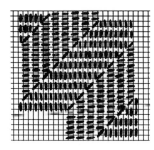

k jacquard cording

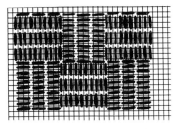

i chessboard
   filling

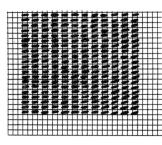

l cording

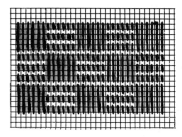

j satin stitch
   and cording

Because the fabric is distorted to make the stitches, it is necessary to work in a frame in order to keep the work flat. The thread is pulled up tight after every stitch to keep the displacement of the ground fabric regular. Finishing off stitches at the end of each row to maintain the correct tension sometimes requires a little ingenuity. It can often be achieved by taking the thread through the back of a stitch on the previous row.

Stitches are carried right up to the outline of the design, any irregularity being covered by the outline stitch.

As there can be no knots showing, all threads are started and finished by darning into the back of other stitches. The first thread used is started with a knot on the surface of the fabric, the knot being cut off and the end darned in when other threads have provided a framework.

167

Variations of drawn fabric embroidery have come from as far afield as India and Dresden in Germany. It was very fashionable on heavy linen in the eighteenth century, and on fine muslins in the late eighteenth and the nineteenth century, when it adorned the dress of fine ladies and of infants. Work of this second period can easily be recognized by the delicate floral designs used, such as the spray from a child's christening robe in *fig. 167*. Here almost all the outlines were in satin stitch or cording (*fig 169*).

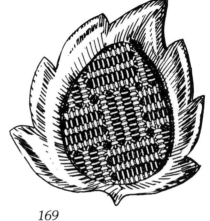

169

The clean edges and high surface of the satin stitch were achieved by padding. First an outline was worked in a very tight chain stitch. The interior of the shape was then filled with satin stitch, often several layers, worked at right angles to the final stitches, and finally the top surface was worked. The needle would be brought up from beneath the surface of the fabric, tight against the chain stitch and in an angle away from it, so that the stitch was almost hidden under the edge of the chain. It would be then taken down the other side at a similarly sharp angle (*fig. 170*). A floss cotton or linen was used for the satin stitch, instead of the corded thread used for the drawn fabric stitches.

168

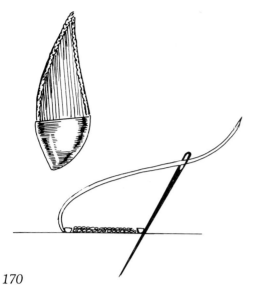

170

Stems were worked in cording or trailing. A thick thread or a bundle of threads was secured at the beginning of a line, and then held in one hand while a soft floss was worked over it, binding it down on the line with a stitch which came up and went down in the same hole so that the round cord appeared to lie on the line instead of being part of it (*fig. 171*).

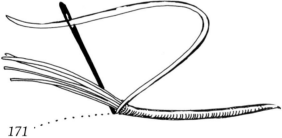

171

Sharp-pointed, large-eyed crewel needles would be used for the surface embroidery, as the threads of the ground fabric would need to be pierced instead of pushed aside in this instance.

Project 8: Table mat and napkin in jacquard stitch

Frame up a piece of coarse evenweave linen, 20 threads to 2.5 cm (1 in.). The napkin will require a piece at least 40 cm (16 in.) square, and the table mat a piece 40 × 50 cm (16 × 20 in.). Tack a line in a contrasting colour to indicate the finished size of each – 30 × 30 cm (12 × 12 in.) and 30 × 40 cm (12 × 16 in.).

Using a coton à broder or coton perlé thread to match the fabric, count 12 threads in from one corner and work 14 lines of Jacquard cording to fill the corner of the napkin (*fig. 172*). Remove the napkin from the frame and complete in the hand.

On the line which has been tacked to indicate the edge, work a line of hedebo buttonhole stitch

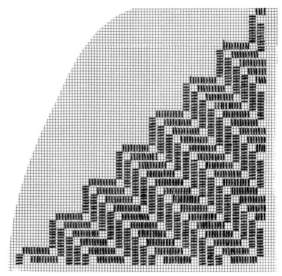

172

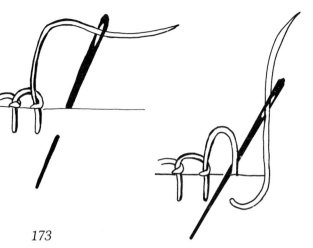

173

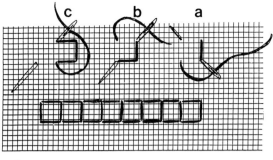

175

The mat is worked in a similar fashion, but allowance must be made for a row of ringed backstitch (*fig. 176*) and a further row of four-sided

(*fig. 173*). Pushing aside the threads, work four buttonhole stitches over four threads, leave four threads, and work four more buttonhole stitches (*fig. 174*).

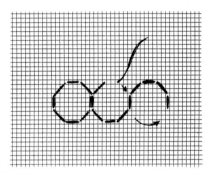

176

stitch between the jacquard pattern and the border, being 32 threads in all. Finish as for the napkin.

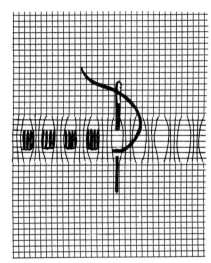

174

Be sure to start at the corner where the jacquard stitch has been worked, so that any necessary adjustments can be made away from the pattern.

When this has been worked all the way around the napkin, fold the edges over and work four-sided stitch through both thicknesses, all the way round (*fig. 175*). Work another two rows and trim off the surplus fabric from the back of the napkin.

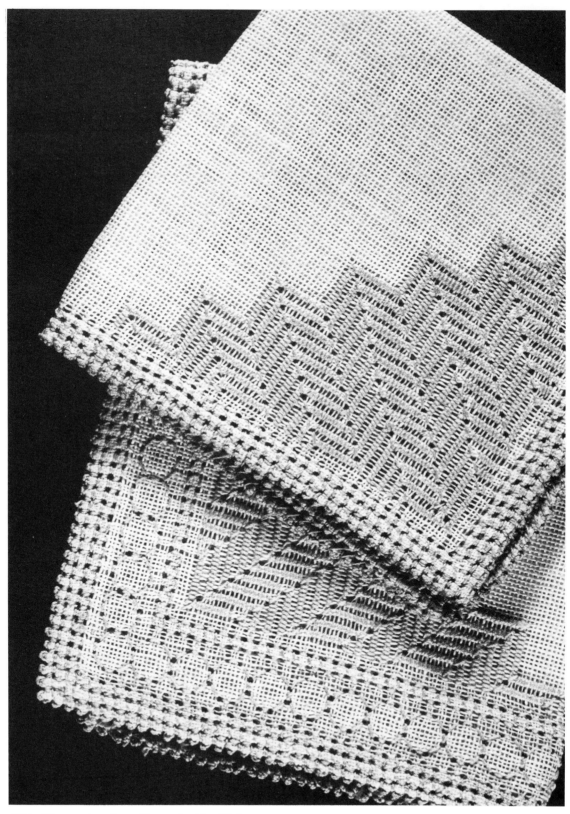

177 *Placemat and napkin worked by Jill Jones.*

Project 9:
Traycloth with wild roses

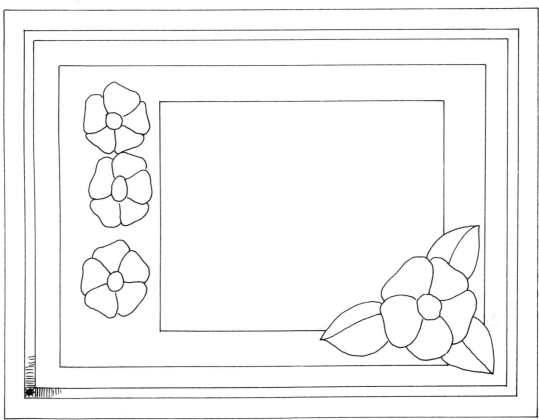

178

Frame up a piece or evenweave linen, 30 threads to 2.5 cm (1 in.). The finished traycloth will be 30 × 40 cm (12 × 16 in.), and an ample hem allowance is necessary.

Trace the pattern for your traycloth (*fig. 178*) on to tissue paper and pin this to the cloth, lining up the straight lines with the grain of the fabric. Tack the design through paper and cloth with a thread of contrasting colour. Tear the tissue paper away.

I regret to say that some impatient people have been known to draw the design directly on to the framed-up linen using a quilter's or dressmaker's marking pen, the ink of which is supposed to vanish with the application of a drop of water. Unfortunately, while this is indeed the case with cotton, on linen it can sometimes leave an ugly brown mark which will not yield to household bleaches. In despair, I cast around for any remedy, however unlikely, and found that the application of a solution of sodium metabisulphite (campden

tablets) removed all traces. Another good reason for having a winemaker in the family!

Next, proceed to work the filling stitches. The background border is worked in step stitch, (*fig. 179*); the top rose in faggot stitch; the second in the

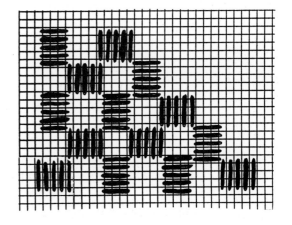

179

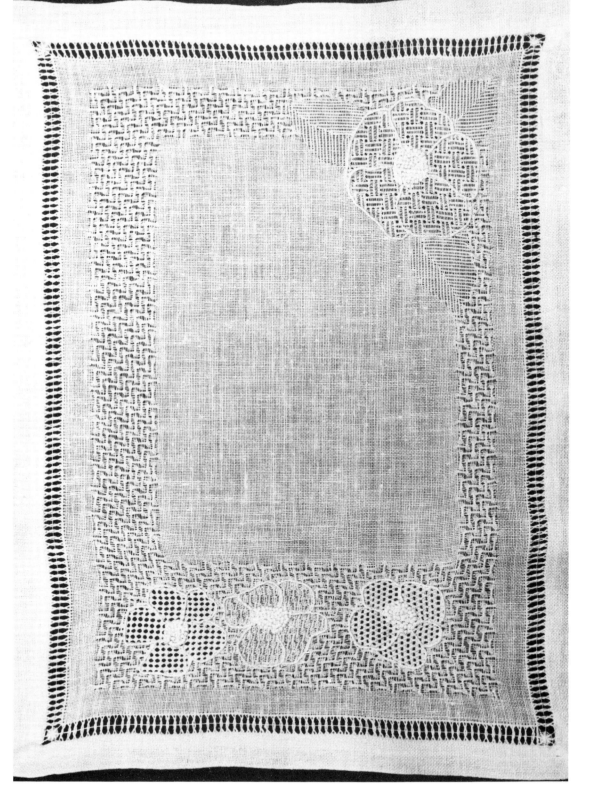

180

satin stitch and cording shown in *fig. 166j*; the third in wave stitch, *fig. 166a*; while the large rose is worked in chessboard filling, *fig. 166i*. The leaves are worked in cording, *166l*.

The hem of the traycloth is worked as shown in Chapter 6. All outlines were worked in whipped chain stitch (*fig. 181*).

181

It is possible to work drawn fabric embroidery on machine-made fabrics which are not truly evenweave. It can look well, for instance, on fine wool fabrics, and if a toning instead of a matching colour is used, can be most effective on clothing.

182

Besides the stitches already given there are literally dozens of others which can be used (*fig. 183*).

183

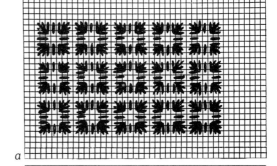

a

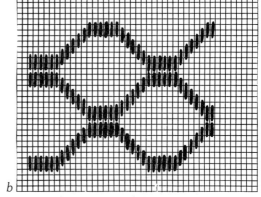

b

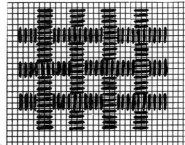

c

Further reading
Esther Fangel, Ida Winckler and Agnete W. Madsen, *Danish Pulled Thread Embroidery*, Dover Publications
Moyra McNeill, *Pulled Thread*, Bell & Hyman
Edna Wark, *Drawn Fabric Embroidery*, Batsford

EIGHT

Drawn ground work

Quite a number of traditional styles of embroidery rely for their effect on a silhouette of linen standing out from a lacy background. This background is sometimes worked in drawn or pulled fabric stitches, sometimes in drawn thread work, but as there is considerable overlap between these two kinds of embroidery, and the effect achieved is distinctive, I think it is reasonable to include them under the title of 'drawn ground work'.

Russian drawn thread work (sometimes called Russian drawn ground)

Traditionally worked on a closely woven, evenweave linen, using a matching thread for the embroidery, the shape of the motif is first transferred to the linen, and the outline is then worked in heavy chain stitch (fig. 184).

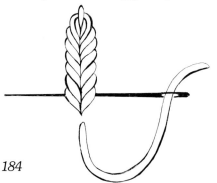

184

In some cases the inside of this motif is also embroidered with surface stitches which rely on the grid of the evenweave, geometric patterns of satin stitch and pattern darning being most common, sometimes embellished with four-sided stitch and herringbone (fig. 186).

The outside of the area to be defined is now outlined with embroidery, either buttonhole stitch or Russian herringbone stitch, which is a herringbone worked over seven threads vertically, and multiples of nine and three threads horizontally, as shown in fig. 185.

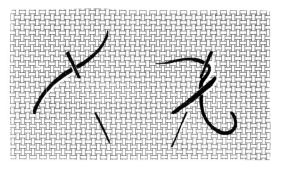

185

When both inner and outer outlines have been worked, the fabric is released from the frame and the unwanted threads cut away. This is done from the back of the work, using very sharp scissors and great care. Two threads are cut; two are left across the whole area to be drawn, both horizontally and

186

vertically, and the loose threads drawn out (*fig. 187*). The work is put back into the frame again to work the ground.

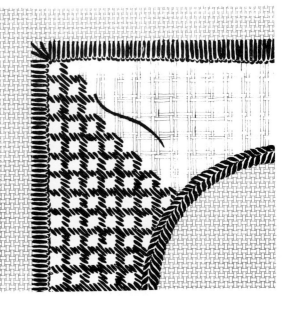

187

109

188

Fig. 188 shows a cat which could be worked in this fashion, using linen or cotton threads which match the colour of the ground fabric.

There is another kind of Russian drawn thread work which has the ground area outlined with buttonhole stitch, and the whole area drawn and overcast with a lighter-weight thread and fewer stitches (fig. 189).

The motif, which has been worked out on graph paper, is then darned into the ground, using the same thread as has been used for overcasting.

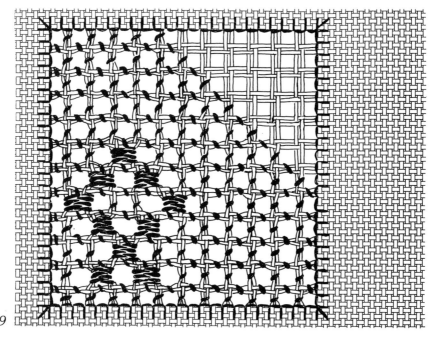

189

190

Sicilian drawn thread work

This can easily be confused with Russian drawn ground. Again, there are two variations on the theme. In the first, which is thought to be older, dating back at least to the fifteenth century, the ground is drawn out in multiples of four threads, but the darning back is done before the threads are corded (*fig. 191*).

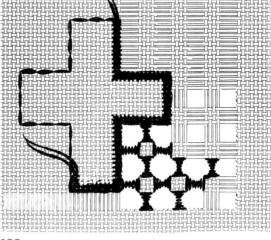

192

In the later style the work has the design first worked in double back stitch (Holbein stitch), outlined in corded satin stitch, and the background threads then drawn and corded (*fig. 192*).

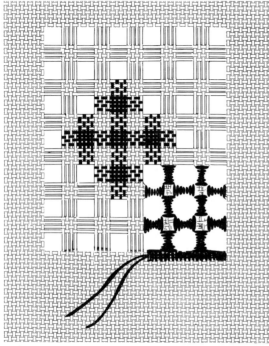

191

Rodi

Another Italian embroidery, known as Rodi work, has a drawn fabric background instead of drawn thread.

The motif is first outlined in a firm stitch, commonly stem stitch (*fig. 193*), although chain stitch (*fig.194*) is found in some examples.

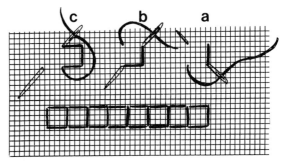

195

The background is then worked in four-sided stitch (*fig. 195*).

Since no threads are withdrawn from the fabric, no outline stitches are required at the edge of the ground area, but as this stitch draws the fabric out of shape, great care must be taken to ensure that it is firmly secured in the frame before the embroidery is commenced, and kept drum-tight whilst being worked. It is almost impossible to pull distorted fabric back into shape afterwards if it has been allowed to get slack while working.

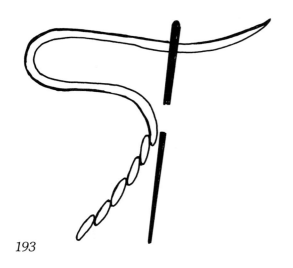

193

Castelguidi

In Castelguidi embroidery the whole surface of the background is worked in double faggot stitch (*fig. 196*), the surface embroidery which decorates it being superimposed upon the finished ground.

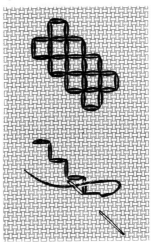

196

The motifs are worked in a manner which gives them a strong texture. Lines are worked in padded stem stitch (*fig. 197*), where a sheaf of threads is

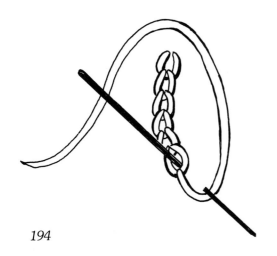

194

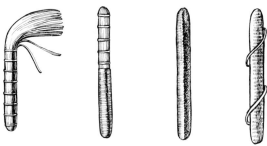

197

laid upon the background and caught down with overcasting. Satin stitch is then worked over this bundle, the ends being neatened and secured. The whole is covered with lines of stem stitch, worked by picking up two or three threads of the satin stitch (the number should be constant) and working from bottom to top. Worked carefully, this will give a very firm round bar which can be further decorated with cording, if required.

Old examples of Castelguidi embroidery almost invariably have patterns based on flowers. Little flowers are worked in detached buttonhole stitch (*fig. 199*). Straight stitch is worked in lines enclosing a hexagon or a pentagon, and the detached

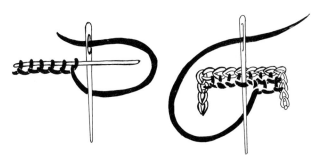

199

buttonhole is worked, loose, over the bars thus formed. The 'petals' decrease in size as the work progresses, until only one or two stitches remain. These are brought to the centre and the 'petal' secured with a line of curl stitch (*fig. 200*).

200

Further decoration is added with curl stitch (*fig. 201a*) – a tightly whipped backstitch, – and buttonhole bars (*b*) worked over straight stitch.

198

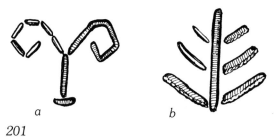

a   b

201

To illustrate the difference between Rodi and Castelguidi embroidery, I have worked two samples. Having grown up on a sheep farm in Saskatchewan, I have enjoyed returning to 'sheep country' on moving recently from London to Northamptonshire, and decided to celebrate the

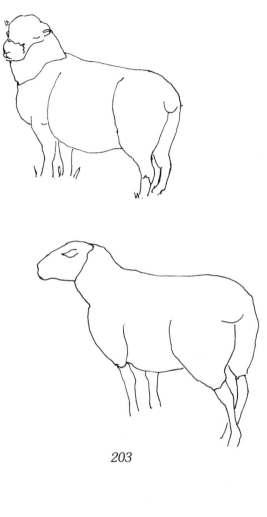

203

202

fact. I made a sketch of sheep (*fig. 202*), simplified it (*fig. 203*), and then worked one of the sheep first in Rodi embroidery (*fig 204*) and then in Castelguidi (*fig. 205*), where the detached buttonhole stitch gave a satisfactorily woolly effect.

204

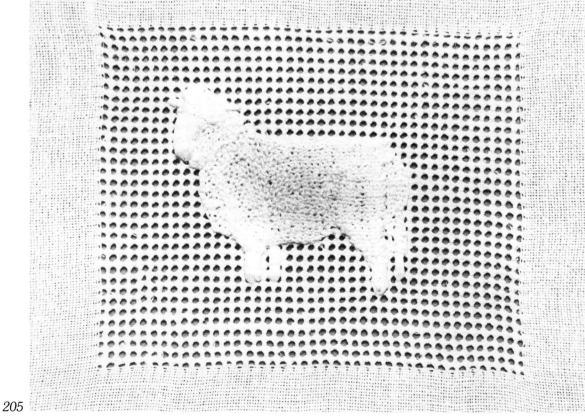

205

116

Hedebo embroidery

Whilst hedebo is not a drawn ground embroidery, it fits best into this chapter because of the similarity in the manner of working. In the earlier forms of hedebo embroidery the motifs were drawn, and the rest of the embroidery worked in surface stitchery. (In later forms, evenweave linen was frequently replaced by much more tightly woven linen, and patterns were achieved by cutting shapes and filling them with needlemade laces.)

Hedebo embroidery is a traditional Danish craft, and was worked first on homespun and woven linen. The motif was transferred to the linen, the outlines worked in chain stitch, and all surface embroidery completed before the work was removed from the frame to cut the ground, working from the back of the material (*fig. 206*). The grounds were, for the most part, worked over a grid of two threads left and two drawn, either corded or lightly corded and woven (*fig. 207*), in much the same manner as that used for Russian drawn ground.

206

117

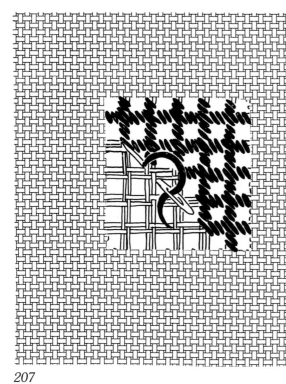

207

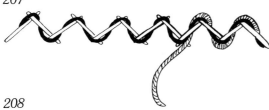

208

Further embellishment was added with woven herringbone stitch (*fig. 208*) and buttonholed eyelets (*fig. 209*).

209

Work was finished with hemstitched or needlewoven lines (*fig. 210*).

210

118

Project 10: Suntop
with hedebo embroidery

Although hedebo embroidery is generally associated with household linen, it can be used to great advantage on dress. Instructions are given here for a linen suntop with a panel of hedebo embroidery.

The pattern is illustrated on a 2.5 cm (1 in.) grid, and will fit a size 12—14. *Fig. 212* shows the front of the top, with the pattern in position, and an optional casing for elastic at waist level.

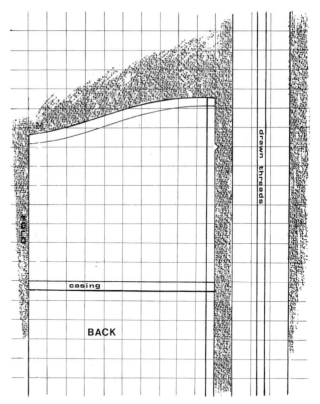

212

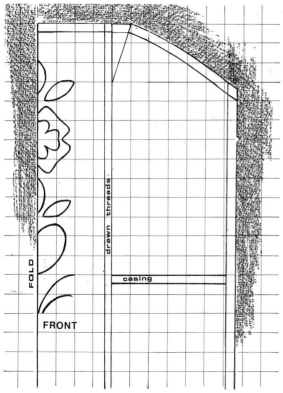

211

Ten threads are drawn out at the edge of the dart, and hemstitched with ladder stitch, catching in the fold of the dart to the hemstitched line. The centre of the back dips slightly to the centre back fold.

The embroidery should be worked before the suntop is cut out. It is advisable to mark the seam lines before you start, preferably by tacking them with a contrasting thread. The pattern for the embroidery is shown in *fig. 213*.

213

119

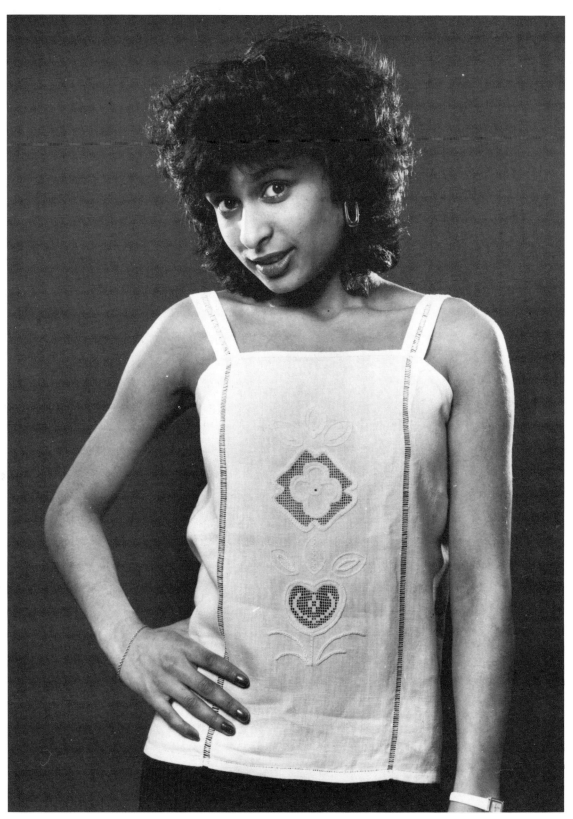

To make the suntop, join the underarm seams with a french seam or a flat felled seam (so there are no raw edges left to fray), and then turn over and hemstitch a small hem at top and bottom edges.

The two shoulder straps have 10 threads drawn out down the centre, and the edges turned under and hemstitched to form ladders. One end of each strap is fastened neatly to the inside of the top of the ladder on the suntop, the other end being arranged as required to provide a good fit.

If the suntop is to be gathered at the waist, stitch a casing in place on the wrong side of the garment, from the left ladder at the front, around the back, ending at the right ladder. Insert elastic and secure.

Further reading

Herta Puls, *The Art of Cutwork and Appliqué*, Batsford

Margaret Swain, *Ayrshire and Other Whitework*, Shire Publications
The Flowerers: The Story of Ayrshire White Needlework, W. & R. Chambers

NINE

Cutwork on evenweave fabric

Another family of embroideries on evenweave linen is that where areas of the fabric are cut away and spaces are either left open or embellished with needlemade laces.

Hardanger embroidery

One of the most widely known forms is hardanger embroidery. This type of openwork originated around the Hardanger Fjord in Norway, but has become popular much farther afield. It combines cut thread, patterns in satin stitch, needleweaving, needle lace, and some pulled stitches to make geometrical patterns which are quite distinctive.

The designs are based upon multiples of the kloster block. A central square is outlined by rows of satin stitch worked over an even number of threads (giving an uneven number of stitches). One row is worked vertically (*fig. 215*), the work then

215

being turned and a second row worked at right angles to the first (*fig. 216*). The first stitch of the

216

second row is worked in the same hole as the last stitch of the first row. The embroidery is continued until a square has been completed.

With sharp, pointed scissors, cut out the square of fabric enclosed by the satin stitch, making sure that the embroidered stitches are not nicked. The resulting figure is a kloster block (*fig. 217*).

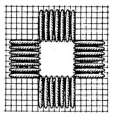

217

Hardanger designs are built up with groups and variations of these kloster blocks, sometimes decorated with needlemade lace or needleweaving, sometimes left plain. The simplest decorated treatment is shown in *fig. 218*.

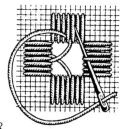

218

Larger motifs can be made by satin stitching over more threads, and then cutting four holes, leaving a woven centre with loose threads joining it to the sides of the square. The example in *fig. 219* shows the loose threads being worked in needleweaving

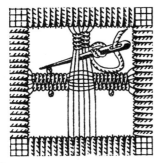

219

with picots, while *fig. 219* demonstrates a method of finishing a square where the loose threads have

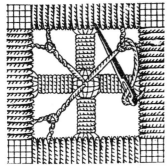

220

been whipped into cords. Centres of such squares are also often decorated with woven or whipped wheels (spider's webs), shown in *fig. 221*.

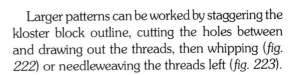

Larger patterns can be worked by staggering the kloster block outline, cutting the holes between and drawing out the threads, then whipping (*fig. 222*) or needleweaving the threads left (*fig. 223*).

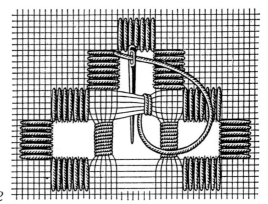

222

223

Further decoration is added with four-sided stitch (*fig. 224*), double running stitch (*fig. 225*),

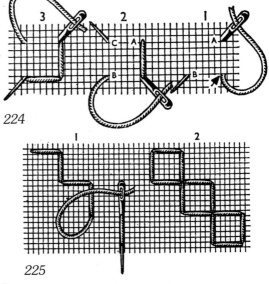

224

225

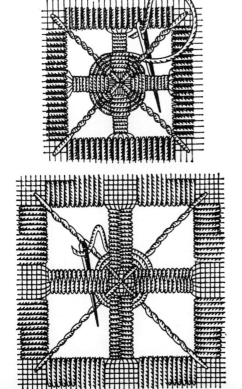

221

123

eyelets, (*fig. 226*), or blocks of satin stitch (*fig. 227*).

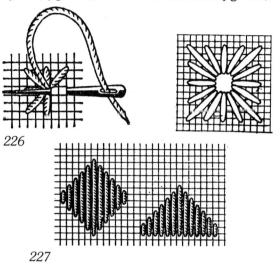

226

227

228

Hardanger embroidery can be worked on any firmly woven evenweave material, but a special fabric is sold for it. This has a double weave, but the two threads lying together are treated as one when working the embroidery.

Whilst, traditionally, hardanger embroidery has been employed for household linen, it can also be used to decorate clothing. A chart is given in *fig. 229* for working the child's yoke in *fig. 228*.

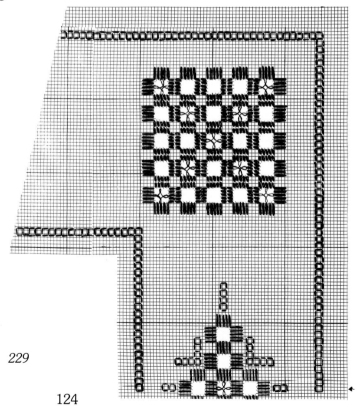

229

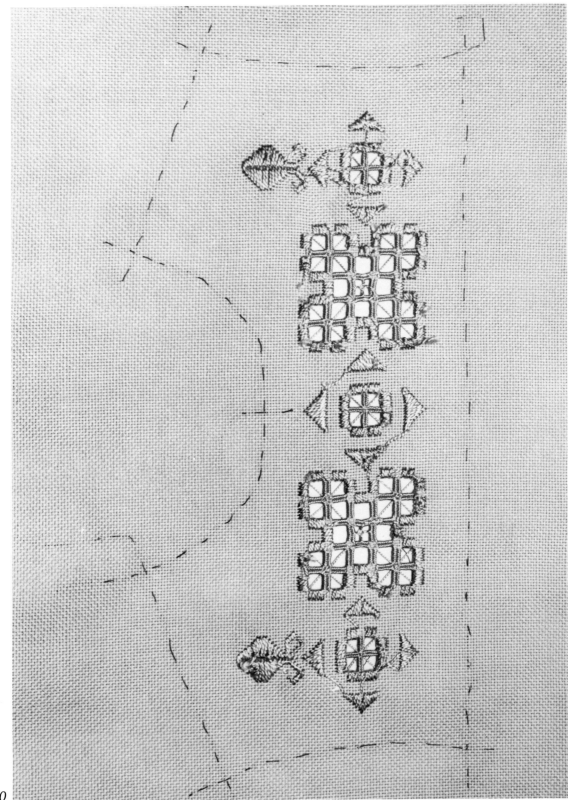

This yoke is to fit a six-year-old, the darker squares on the graph paper indicating the square inch (2.5 cm) of the pattern on 22-threads-to-the-inch hardanger fabric (double threads).

Fig. 230 shows treatment in hardanger embroidery for a more rounded style of yoke.

Italian cutwork

This work consists of small squares or rectangles cut from evenweave linen, over which designs are worked in needleweaving and buttonhole stitch. It closely resembles reticella lace, but threads from the fabric are actually incorporated, whereas in reticella the foundation threads are stitched to a card before working over them. The resulting lace is then cut away from the card and inserted into a linen which need not be evenweave.

In Italian cutwork the area to be worked is outlined with a running stitch, the edges are secured with satin stitch, which may be corded for extra strength, and the threads are then cut away and withdrawn, leaving a centre cross as a base for the embroidery (*fig. 231*).

The central bars are strengthened and decorated with needleweaving, diagonal threads are taken from the corners to the centre and back, and whipped, and further decoration is added with buttonhole stitch and picots.

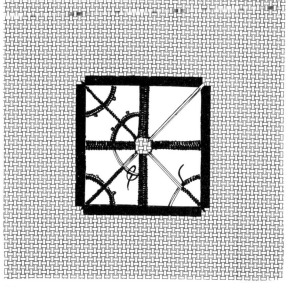

232

Other decoration is added to the embroidery with outlines in four-sided stitch (*fig. 224*), three-sided stitch (*fig. 233*) and hemstitched and

233

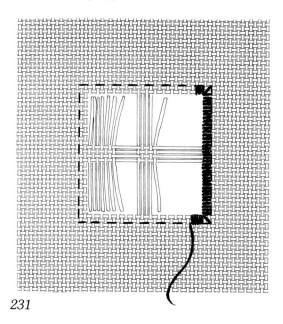

231

234

needlewoven bands. Sometimes the surface is further embellished with surface stitchery in bullion knots (*fig. 234*) and cording or trailing (*fig. 171*).

Very similar embroideries will be found under the headings of Lakeland or Ruskin work, Greek lace work, and Aemilia Ars.

Further reading
Œnone Cave, *Cutwork Embroidery and How to do it*, Dover
Elizabeth Prickett, *Ruskin Lace and Linen Work*, Batsford
Herta Puls, *The Art of Cutwork and Appliqué*, Batsford

—— TEN ——

Design and experiment

All the embroideries described so far have been confined each to its own area of work, with no mixing of media, and for the most part, the designs have been traditional. For me, however, much of the enjoyment of embroidery lies in experiment and the pushing back of frontiers.

To begin with, whilst I agree that copying is the easiest way of learning a technique when starting, it can make for a very drab existence if one doesn't progress beyond this stage. Painted and trammed canvases are fine for the person who has never threaded a needle before, but no-one can say, with any real honesty, 'That's my work – I did that!', when pointing to a completed kit. I find that working a flower 'painting' in petit point on silk

mesh can become very dreary and boring, even when I have designed the picture myself, and can change it as I work if I so wish – so how much more dreary must be the 'Gainsborough' or 'Lowry' worked entirely in tent stitch! I don't think I could resist the temptation to change at least the background stitches. I see no reason why one should be restricted even to one family of stitches when working a panel.

The untimely end of some much-loved elms resulted in the collection of vast quantities of bits of bark for use in the art rooms at the school where I taught for many years. Some of these strayed into the embroidery room and became the foundation of a panel (*fig. 235*).

235

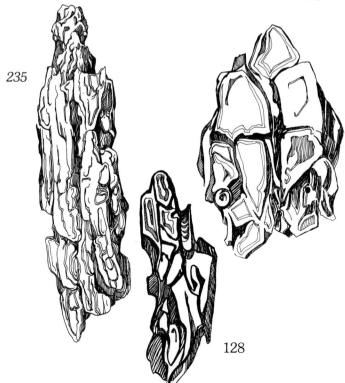

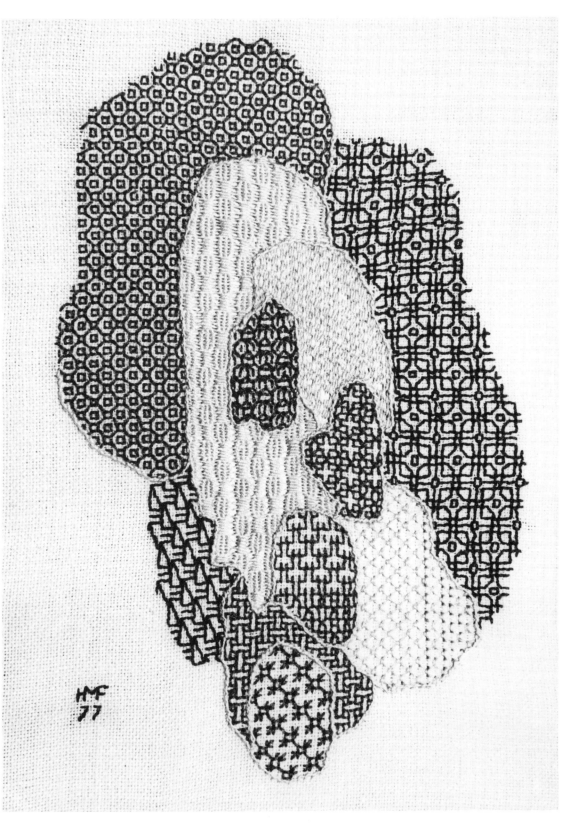

236

129

The blackwork stitches in *fig. 236* were worked in two colours of golden brown, whilst the pulled work was done in a linen thread which matched the background fabric.

'Nimrod the Mighty Hunter', on the front cover, was worked in faggot stitch (*see fig. 237*), using a

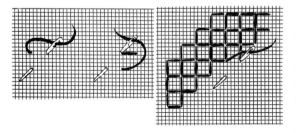

237

linen thread slightly warmer in colour than the background. His eyes are worked in tent stitch in fine silk thread, and the jungle around him is worked in cross stitch using various weights of silk thread.

The extremely elaborate Christmas card in *fig. 239* (it is surprising what one will do when a competition is arranged!) has tent stitch worked in silk for the holly, pulled work using a very fine coton perlé, and outlines in corded satin stitch, padded satin stitch, and chain stitch. The fabric was mounted over silver plastic material to give an added Christmas glitter.

A walk through a larch wood in Austria, followed by an afternoon of pouring rain, resulted in some detailed drawings of the fungus which hangs from dead branches or lies on the forest floor (*fig. 238*).

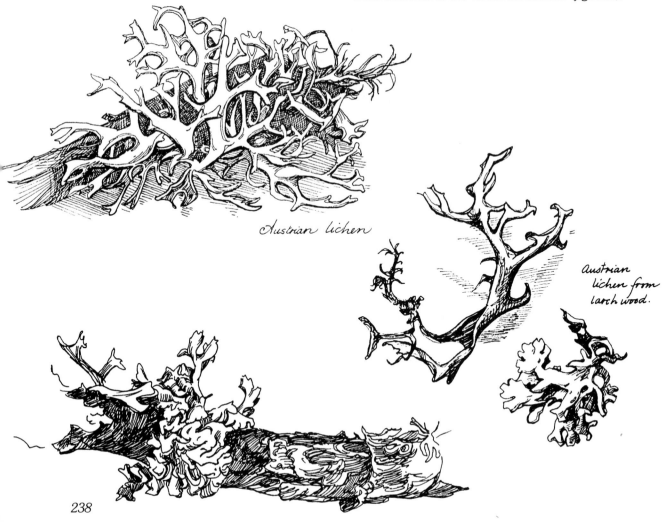

Austrian lichen

Austrian lichen from larch wood.

238

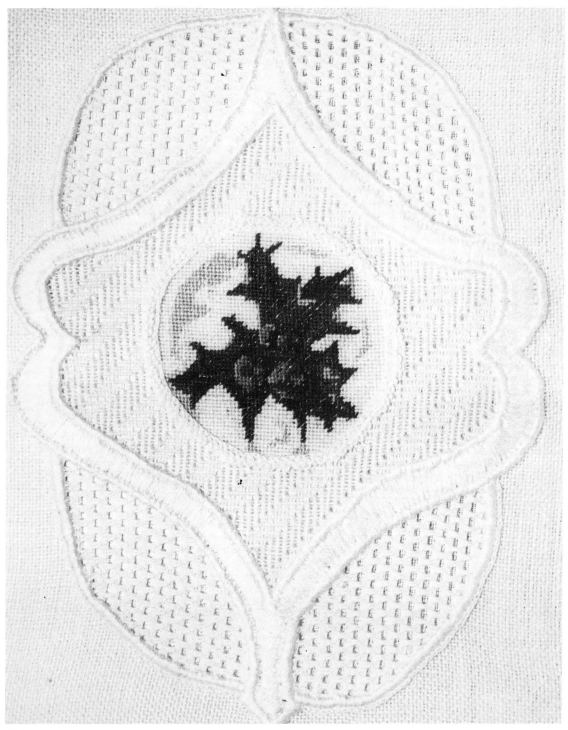

239

240

Over some months these sketches slowly
evolved in my imagination until I started work on
the panel in *fig. 240* (also shown in colour pl. 11).

The forest floor is represented by florentine
embroidery worked in shades of green and brown
to the pattern shown in *fig. 101*, with the fungus
built up on it using other canvas work stitches, and
padded appliqué in leather, plastic and fabric. It is
further enriched by the use of raised chain band
(*fig. 241*), Portuguese border stitch (*fig. 242*), and
couched metal threads.

242

241

132

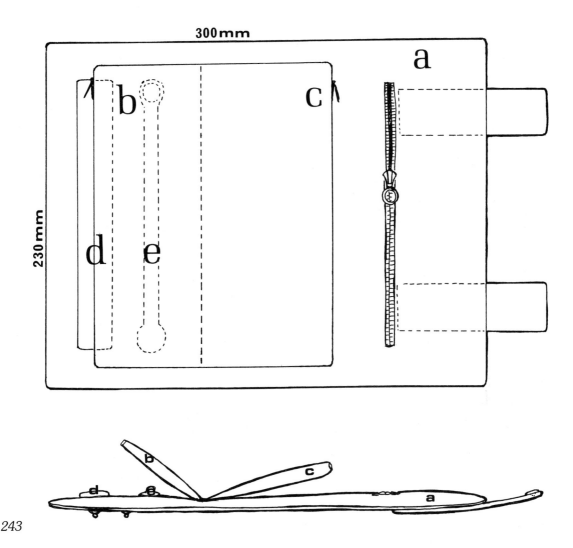

300 mm

230 mm

a

b

c

d

e

243

When working the travelling jewellery case shown in colour pl. 12, a diagram for which is given in *fig. 243*, I used a design based on crystal forms, but incorporated leather appliqué into the design, as well as using stranded cotton, woollen threads, raffia and chenille for the stitching. Suede was used for the lining, with an inner lining of silk against the back of the canvas work embroidery.

I stitched the pieces of the suede lining by hand, using a glover's needle (chisel-bladed) and linen thread. The ring bearer was formed over a heavy cord, and the end which is caught down by a snap fastener was lined with suede and the edges reinforced with buttonhole stitch. The inner pockets were made separately, and then stitched in place.

In *fig. 243*, *a* is a large pocket for necklets, chains, etc.; *b* and *c* are small pockets with zip fasteners along their top edges. (Sew the zips into the two ends of the rectangles of suede. Turn to the wrong side and sew up the sides. Turn out and stitch the pocket thus formed to the outside of pocket *a*, making two small pockets for earrings, etc.) *d* is a brooch holder, stitched down at both ends, and *e* the ring carrier, attached by a snap fastener at one end only, and stitched securely at the other.

The lower drawing shows a view of the case. The tabs are fixed on after the whole case is complete, and have snap fasteners which fix on to two different positions, depending upon whether the case is empty or full.

Were I to make another such case, it would be an

133

244

interesting exercise to base the design on natural forms and work a modified florentine design, experimenting with the patterns on leaves of cyclamen (*see fig. 244*), or, perhaps, using patterns from the wings of a moth to provide the starting point for a design (*fig. 245*).

Needleweaving need not be confined to the threads of table linen. Try working with scrim or hessian, or even with threads stitched in place across the fabric. The small panel in *fig. 246* has as its background a piece of silk left over from experiments with batik made years ago, with threads withdrawn from the crash, and woven back using a variety of exotic threads, adding beads for emphasis. The foliage at the top is knotted chenille, couched down with matching silk thread.

245

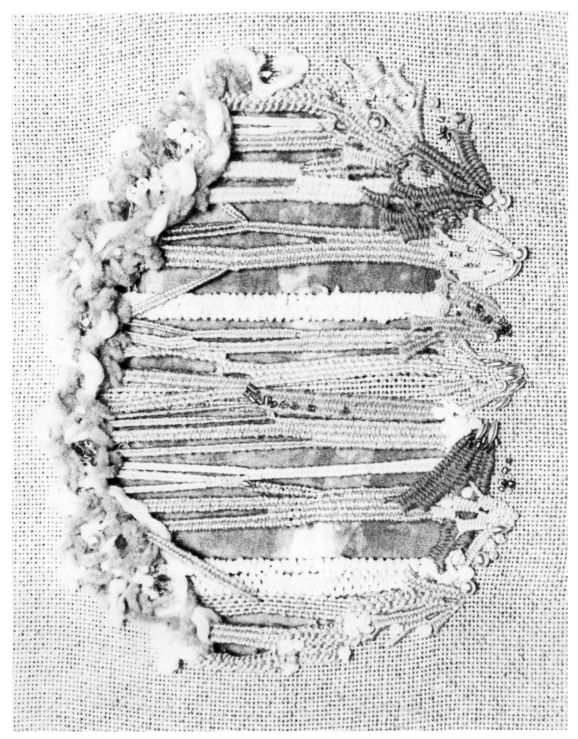

246

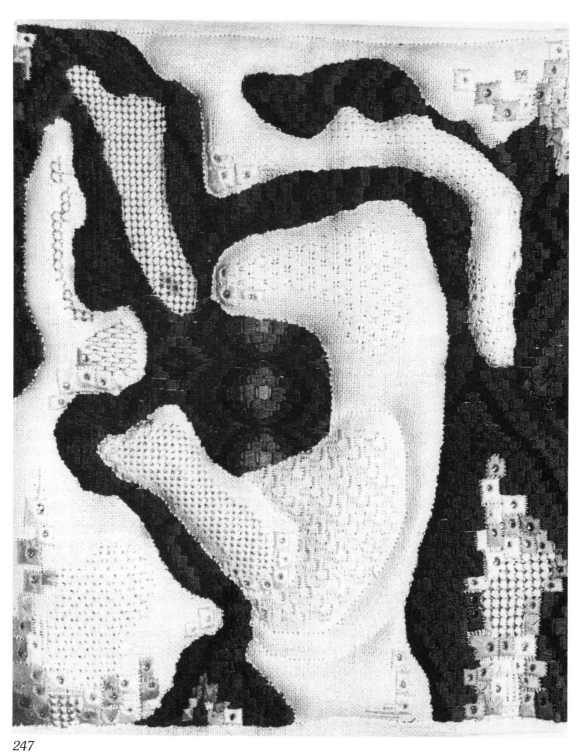

247

The panel in *fig. 247* is based on photographs and sketches of an ice pool we found on a Sunday morning walk along a nearby lane after a sharp frost. The combination of pulled fabrics in silk thread with the rich colours and shapes of florentine embroidery is enhanced by the use of a woven lurex fabric behind the pulled work, coupled with trapunto quilting (where the backing fabric is slit, the area padded with a suitable wadding, and the slit then sewn up again, leaving a raised area on the front of the piece to catch the light and provide a third dimension).

It seems likely that I will find other uses for my sketches of the ice pond in future embroidery projects (*see fig. 248*), while collections and

248

drawings of agates (*fig. 249*) have unlimited possibilities for design.

If your eyes are open, inspiration for embroidery is everywhere about us, once the techniques have been mastered. I only hope that I have opened doors for you to a pastime which has given me immense pleasure over a great many years.

249

Further reading
Jan Beaney, *The Young Embroiderer*, Nicholas Kaye
Jan Messent, *Embroidery and Nature*, Batsford
Betty Whyatt and Joan Oxland, *Design for Embroidery*, Mills and Boon
Plus any children's books illustrated by Carole Barker (e.g. *The Bald Twit Lion* by Spike Milligan)

Suppliers

UK

The Campden Needlecraft Centre
High Street
Chipping Campden
Gloucestershire

de Denne Limited
159/161 Kenton Road
Kenton
Harrow
Middlesex HA3 0EU

Irish Linen Depot
39 Bond Street
Ealing W5 5AS
Tel. 01-576 2488

Mace and Nairn
89 Crane Street
Salisbury
Wiltshire SP1 2PY

Needle Needs
20 Beauchamp Place
Knightsbridge
London SW3 1NQ

The Nimble Thimble
26 The Green
Bilton
Rugby
Warwickshire

Christine Riley
53 Barclay Street
Stonehaven
Kincardineshire AB3 2AR

The Royal School of Needlework
25 Princes Gate
London SW7 1QE

A. Sells
'Lane Cove'
49 Pedley Lane
Clifton
Shefford
Bedfordshire
(Lacemaking equipment)

(These are all suppliers who I have used and can personally recommend. If you feel you need more, the directory of shops in *Embroidery* magazine, published by the Embroiderers' Guild of Great Britain, may be useful.)

USA

American Crewel and Canvas Studio
PO Box 453
Canastota
NY 13031

Craft Gallery Ltd
PO Box 541
New City
NY 10956

Cross Patch, Inc.
8359 Creedmore Road
Towne North Plaza
Raleigh
NC 27612

Mary McGregor
PO Box 2555
Salisbury
Maryland 21801
(Canvas work yarns)

The Needlecraft Shop
PO Box 1406
Canoga Park
CA 91304

The World in Stitches
PO Box 198
Osgood Roda
Milford
NH 03055

Canada

One Stitch at a Time
102A Main Street
PO Box 114
Picton
Ontario
K0K 2TO

Index